Praise for Alliances and Co-Evolution

'Much of the – now vast – literature on business alliances has focused upon globalized mass manufacturing industries or upon hi-tech sectors such as semiconductors or pharmaceutical products. This book is a refreshing change in that it looks at the "Age of alliances" through the lens of a traditional service sector: banking. Serious students and practitioners of banking/finance, and of strategic management, would be well advised to read it, to comprehend the massive, and multi-faceted, nature of the "alliance revolutions" in the financial services sector. The significance of this book, however, goes far beyond this. Dr ul-Haq introduces new notions to alliance analysis in general. In particular, he makes a distinction (i) between "infrastructure" and "strategic" alliances, and (ii) between various forms of "co-evolution" in alliances. These new concepts are of immensely wider significance than that "merely" of the global financial services sector. For example, the contemporary debate about the nature, and future, of the European Union can be seen as one about whether it is, or should be, an infrastructure or strategic alliance. Moreover, Dr ul-Haq's co-evolution analysis is of wide applicability: not only as regards business firms, but also political parties and coalitions, and even alliances between organized criminal enterprises. I suspect, therefore, that this is one of those books which – although seemingly focused up a particular sector – will, eventually, have a *much* wider impact on the social and managerial "arts" and sciences generally, through its introduction of valuable new analytical concepts.' – **Professor John Burton,** *formerly Birmingham Business School, University of Birmingham, UK*

'In this extremely well-presented monograph, the author, Dr ul-Haq, generously shares with fellow-students as well as with advanced practitioners the rich fruits of his extensive reading, theoretical understanding and penetrating practical insights. His sure-footed analysis comes to life with a fascinating wealth of evidence drawn from painstaking personal interviews and questionnaires. The result is an exciting presentation of the unsuspected ways that Adam Smith's apparently simple precept of the division of labour leads on to varied and intricate patterns of collaboration between otherwise independent companies.

Some of these strategic alliance arrangements are for narrow, specific, short-term purposes, while others develop more widely and may even lead to a full-blown merger or take-over. This study illustrates from the dynamic world of local, national and international banking how both entrepreneurial bankers and their customers can benefit from carefully specified forms of corporate cooperation in an increasingly competitive universe which is here to stay.' – **Lord Harris of High Cross,** *Cross Bench Member of the House of Lords, Former Founding Chairman of the Institute of Economic Affairs, London, UK*

'Dr Rehan ul-Haq has published a unique book that combines considerable detail about banking operations and inter-bank alliances with an exhaustive coverage of theory on inter-firm cooperation. It is at once a review of the evolution of the banking sector and banking history, as well as a life-cycle approach to understanding alliances from their negotiation stage, to joint management, to their eventual dissolution. Dr ul-Haq's work reveals an impressive ability to marshal the growing academic literature on alliances, as well as scholarly papers from Economics and Organization Management, while applying these concepts to banking strategy. A deep, scholarly monograph which will be appreciated by students of inter-organizational cooperation, the book could also be highly rewarding to the erudite banker or strategist. In the empirical aspect of the book, Dr ul-Haq draws on 23 years of secondary data in the banking sector, on a questionnaire sent to 217 banks in 20 European nations, as well as on interviews. This range of empirical approaches, the deeply-considered sweep of theory, and what appears to be considerable knowledge of the banking sector and its evolution make this a unique compilation.' – **Farok J. Contractor**, *Professor of International Management, Rutgers Business School, USA*

'Dr ul-Haq's book provides a penetrating analysis of strategic alliances informed by his considerable knowledge of the banking sector. His wide review of the literature is of great help to students, while the insights he offers on how alliances evolve over time fill significant gaps in our knowledge.' – **John Child**, *Professor of Commerce, Birmingham Business School, University of Birmingham, UK*

Also by Dr Rehan ul-Haq

Itshert, J. and ul-Haq, R. (2003) International Banking Strategic Alliances: Reflections on BNP/Dresdner, Palgrave Macmillan: London & New York.

Alliances and Co-Evolution

Insights from the Banking Sector

Rehan ul-Haq

First published 2005 by
PALGRAVE MACMILLAN

Palgrave Macmillan in the UK is an imprint of Macmillan Publishers Limited, registered in England, company number 785998, of Houndmills, Basingstoke, Hampshire RG21 6XS.

Palgrave Macmillan in the US is a division of St. Martin's Press LLC, 175 Fifth Avenue, New York, NY 10010.

Palgrave Macmillan is the global academic imprint of the above companies and has companies and representatives throughout the world.

Palgrave® and Macmillan® are registered trademarks in the United States, the United Kingdom, Europe and other countries.

ISBN-13: 978–1–4039–3312–6   hardback
ISBN-10: 1–4039–3312–X   hardback

This book is printed on paper suitable for recycling and made from fully managed and sustained forest sources. Logging, pulping and manufacturing processes are expected to conform to the environmental regulations of the country of origin.

A catalogue record for this book is available from the British Library.

Library of Congress Cataloging-in-Publication Data
ul-Haq, Rehan
   Alliances and co-evolution : insights from the banking sector / Rehan ul-Haq.
      p. cm.
   Includes bibliographical references and index.
   ISBN 1–4039–3312–X
      1. Banks and banking–Europe. 2. Strategic alliances (Business)–Europe. 3. Banks and banking, International. I. Title.
HG2974.H37 2005
332.1′094–dc22   2005042907

Printed and bound by CPI Group (UK) Ltd, Croydon, CR0 4YY

Dedications and Acknowledgements

This book is dedicated to:

- To God for life and liberty.
- To my late father, Zafar ul-Haq FRCS, for instilling the work ethic.
- To my mother, Salmi Z Haq, for unstinting support.
- To my wife, Lubna S Haq, for great encouragement.
- To my daughter, Aaminah S Haq, for giving hope.
- To my Doctoral Supervisors and Directors of Research, Professors Ian C Morison, Peter Lawrence, Barry Howcroft and Ian Davidson.
- To the Senior Bank Directors for their time and insights.
- To the team at Palgrave Macmillan.

There are so many people who need to be acknowledged.

- The many academics who have provided enlightening insights and practical advice regarding this research.
- The many people who have provided encouragement.
- My family and friends, too many to mention individually, who put up with my overwhelming pre-occupation but still provided friendship.

A research book is an undertaking that requires (alongside the academic achievement) the ability to work in a dedicated way and to sustain interest over a long period of time. The support and advice of fellow academics, family, friends and colleagues has made this possible. The most important are the many managers and directors of banks throughout Europe who gave unstintingly of their time and insights in the course of this research. Without them this would not have happened. Thank you.

Contents

List of Tables

List of Appendices Tables

List of Figures

List of Appendices Figures

Preface

Alliances and Co-Evolution

Strategic alliances are a prevalent form of business organization. The critical characteristics of strategic alliances are detailed using Coase (1937) and the resulting definition tested through primary research and the alternative form, the infrastructure alliance posited. The book examines whether strategic alliances add value in the European banking sector through four types of analysis at two levels of engagement – a 23 year historical review (at industry level); a review of over 400 papers in the academic literature; a questionnaire survey (at firm level) and in-depth interviews (at firm level).

Bankers high pre-existing propensity to enter into strategic alliances is determined and three lifecycles, and the underpinning conditions identified – Clubs and Consortium Banks, Bankassurance and the Virtual bank – the latter involving a fundamental change in Coase (1937) enabled by the underpinning technology. Bankers were found to be followers of potential business streams and the strategic alliance was one form of market entry. The questionnaire research, however, identified that European bankers prefer to enter into alliances (as opposed to own branch or M&A) only in countries which had the appropriate supporting conditions such as definable, enforceable and terminable contracts, the provision of accounting information, stable governments and economic freedom. Direct discussions with senior bankers resulted in a number of valuable insights into the conceiving, forming, organizing, evolving and dissolving of alliances.

Further research into the infrastructure alliance, including 'oscillation' between infrastructure and strategic forms is proposed. The Co-Evolution Model of Strategic Alliances is proposed and taxonomy consisting of parallel co-evolution, convergent co-evolution, divergent co-evolution and the subsidiary taxonomy of differential parallel co-evolution, differential convergent co-evolution and differential divergent co-evolution detailed.

This model provides a mechanism for alliance managers to link together environmental change, changing strategic-intents of alliance partners, the nature, form and purpose of the alliance thereby retaining strategic flexibility and continuing to enjoy the benefits of collaboration.

Strategic alliances are found to add value in European banking but this value is contingent on the strength of the business stream, the global, national and industry conditions and the nature of managerial decisions and drive and the ability of the alliance to co-evolve as the partners strategic intents evolve.

Foreword

by
Professor Pierre Dussauge
HEC – School of Management
Paris, France

Strategic alliances have been a topic of investigation for many years now. Early studies on inter-firm collaboration that envision alliances as more than mere collusion date back to the 60s and 70s. In the 80s and 90s, alliances actually emerged as one of the most researched subjects in the field of strategic management. Numerous books and literally hundreds of articles, some academic and others practitioner-oriented, were published on the subject, exploring such issues as (i) what firms form alliances and why, (ii) how should alliances be organized and managed, (iii) how do alliances evolve over time and (iv) what are the performance implications of alliance strategies, among others (see Gulati, 1998 for an overview). With companies continuing to actively collaborate with one another in the early years of the new millennium, and with many answers still to be provided on the above-mentioned questions, the stream of research on alliances seems unlikely to dry out anytime soon.

This, in itself, is enough of a reason to welcome the publication of a new research book on 'Alliances and Co-Evolution: Insights from the Banking Sector'. More importantly, this book and the research by Rehan ul-Haq from which it is derived, fill a surprising gap in the alliance literature. Most of the work on alliances – with the exception of studies on airline alliances, a sector which seems to have captured the attention of academics more than most others – has indeed tended to focus on manufacturing industries, either explicitly or, more often, implicitly. And while there may be a lot in common between alliances in manufacturing and alliances in service sectors, there are undoubtedly also very significant differences. Many of the forces that have driven companies in such manufacturing industries as automobiles, telecommunication equipment, aerospace, computers, pharmaceuticals, etc. to enter into countless collaborative arrangements, many of which are with competitors, are unlikely to play out in exactly the same way in the service sector. Skyrocketing R&D expenses for example are more typical of manufacturing than they are of services; global competition has drastically affected most manufacturing industries while many services have remained somewhat sheltered in their specific domestic settings. Because of these differences between manufacturing industries and services, there is undoubtedly a lot to learn by taking a closer look at alliance strategies implemented by service firms. Indeed, Rehan ul-Haq's new book provides many intriguing new insights on alliances by specifically looking at alliances in the banking sector.

One first intriguing conclusion that Rehan ul-Haq derived from observing banking alliances has to do with the various types of alliances that he identified in this sector. Developing theoretically sound and empirically relevant alliance typologies has indeed been an important facet of alliance research over the last 20 years. Noting that alliances are an extraordinarily heterogeneous phenomenon, authors have suggested many different classifications of alliances (see among others Hennart, 1988; Yoshino and Rangan, 1995; Doz and Hamel, 1998; Dussauge and Garrette, 1999). None of these typologies however comprehensively addresses all the main management issues that get raised whenever firms choose to collaborate rather than to compete. This suggest that we still do not have a deep enough understanding of the various alliance types that firms get involved in. In that respect, by proposing a new perspective on alliance types derived from the observation of collaborative behaviours in the banking sector, i.e. *infrastructure* vs. *strategic* alliances, Rehan ul-Haq provides a fresh look at why firms choose to collaborate and at how this may affect future competition between allies or between members of the alliance and outsiders. Such a typology, which is much more parsimonious than most other categorizations that have been put forth to date, may provide a broader framework that is applicable to manufacturing industries and service sectors alike.

Another major contribution of this book is Rehan ul-Haq's attempt at providing a clear answer, in the specific context of the banking sector, to one of the most important – albeit frustrating – questions about alliances: do alliances create value for those firms that choose to form them? Rehan ul-Haq's conclusion, based on his in-depth knowledge of banking and on the opinions he gathered from bank managers, is unequivocally 'yes'. Though I am willing to agree with him in the particular context of European banking, I might be a little less enthusiastic than he is in a more general perspective. Indeed, I think one of the reasons why it has been so difficult to answer this question in the past is because it is very difficult to disentangle the reasons that lead firms to form alliances from the factors that drive performance. In other words, firms that are more prone to collaborate may be stronger – or weaker – competitors, thus leading to the observation that firms forming alliances outperform – or under perform – others, when in fact collaboration is merely the appropriate behaviour for strong – or weak – firms. In fact, preliminary observations derived from current research suggest that alliances per se may have little specific impact on performance, if those factors that both lead companies to collaborate and drive their performance are taken into account. The conclusions Rehan ul-Haq has arrived at in the banking sector provide us with fresh empirical evidence that will help us disentangle these difficult issues.

Finally, this book is significant contribution to our knowledge and understanding of the banking sector and, as such, is of major interest for those of us interested in how this industry is evolving and adapting to rapid changes in the environment, in particular in the context of Europe. Overall, Rehan ul-Haq has done a superb job of providing us with both intriguing new insights into the strange world of strategic alliances and a valuable account of changes affecting the banking sector in Europe.

References

Gulati, R (1998) 'Alliances and Networks', *Strategic Management Journal*, Vol. 19, 293–317.

Yoshino, M Y and Rangan, U S (1995) *Strategic Alliances*, Harvard Business School Press.

Hennart, J-F (1988) 'A Transaction Costs Theory of Equity Joint Ventures', *Strategic Management Journal*, Vol. 9, 361–74.

Dussauge, P and Garrette, B (1999) *Cooperative Strategy: Competing Successfully through Strategic Alliances*, John Wiley & Sons.

Doz, Y L and Hamel, G (1998) *Alliance Advantage: The Art of Creating Value through Partnering*, Harvard Business School Press.

List of Abbreviations

APACS	Association for Payment Clearing Services
ATM	Automated Teller Machines
BACS	Bulk electronic clearing for direct debits and credits
BNP	Banque Nationale de Paris
BoE	Bank of England
BOS	Bank of Scotland
BZW	Barclays de Zoete Wadd
CCC	Cheque and credit clearing
CEO	Chief Executive Officer
CHAPS	Clearing House Automated Payments System
EBIC	European Banking Industry Committee
EEC	European Economic Community
EJVs	Equity Joint Ventures
EU	European Union
FDI	Foreign Direct Investment
FSA	Financial Services Authority
HNWI	High Net Worth Individual
HR	Human Resources
HSBC	Hong Kong and Shanghai Banking Corporation
IBOS	International Banking-One Solution
ICAs	International Collaborative Arrangements
IJV	International Joint Venture
IMF	International Monetary Fund
IT	Information Technology
JV	Joint Venture
OPEC	Organization of Oil Producing and Exporting Countries
OS	Overseas
M&A	Mergers and Acquisitions
M&S Typology	Miles and Snow Typology
MBA	Master of Business Administration
M-Form	Multi-Divisional Form
MNEs	Multi National Enterprises
NJV	Non Joint Venture
R&D	Research and Development
SMEs	Small and Medium-sized Enterprises

SWIFT	Society of Worldwide Interbank Funds Transfer
U-Form	Unitary Form
UK+CE	United Kingdom and Continental European

1
Introduction, Structure and Subject

Introduction and research question

Strategic alliances are being used to access know-how, products and markets. In the middle of the 'organic growth-strategic alliances-mergers and acquisitions' continuum they provide a method of rapidly addressing business opportunities that arise whilst sharing know-how, costs and risk, as well as reward, with partners.

There is no question as to the popularity of strategic alliances. The key question is:

Do strategic alliances add value?

This research book examines this question through four types of analysis at two levels of engagement – through a 23 year historical review (industry level); through a review of over 400 papers in the academic literature; through a questionnaire survey (at firm level) and through in-depth interviews (at firm level). The industry examined was the European banking industry.

Structure

This book has six chapters. Chapter One considers the nature of the subject under analysis, the strategic alliance, and differentiates this from the infrastructure alliance, both prevalent forms of cooperation in the banking sector. Chapter Two develops a view as to the historical propensity of banks to collaborate. It reports a longitudinal analysis of the forms of collaboration prevalent in this sector between 1960 and 1993 and considers the research question at an industry level. Chapter Three identifies the theoretical underpinnings of strategic alliances and

1

Table 1.1 Structure of Research Book

Chapter Number and Area	1 Introduction	2 Industry Level Lifecycle Findings	3 Theoretical Foundations	4 Firm Level Postal Survey Findings	5 Firm Level Thematic Interview Findings	6 Conclusion Future Research
External/ Internal Focus		External		Internal to Firm and Manager	Internal to Manager and Firm	
Data Source		Economist Financial Times Bank of England	Journal Articles Books – Single Author and Edited Volumes Proceedings	Questionnaires Returned	Interviews Held	
'Lens' or Perspective		Historical	Theoretical	Firms Practice	Managerial Motivations	
Phillips and Pugh (1994) Class	Contribution	Focal Theory (1) Contribution	Focal (2) and Background Theory	Data Theory Contribution	Data Theory Contribution	Contribution

the perspectives adopted by previous research and those employed in this book. Chapter Four sets out the method used to analyze the postal survey responses and reports the findings, relating them to the research question. Chapter Five reports the analyses of the thematically based interviews and relates the findings to the research question. Chapter Six concludes this book and suggests two areas for future research.

So as to be relatively comprehensive and obtain deep insights into the use of strategic alliances in the European banking sector, four lenses or perspectives are used: historical, theoretical, practical and motivational (Chapters Two, Three, Four and Five respectively). Furthermore the focus of inquiry moves from changes in the external context to firm level decision making to the motivations of managers (Chapters Two, Four and Five respectively). Table 1.1 summarizes the structure of this book.

Subject

Strategic alliances – definition and taxonomy

Strategic alliances – definition

Strategic alliance theory is a sub-set of theories governing the structure of organizations. Coase (1937) set out to explain why firms exist – that is, why market based transactions do not in all situations result in the most efficient allocation of resources.

The rationale of the firm (as expounded by Coase and developed by Williamson [1986]) is, at its simplest, that the existence of transaction costs and uncertainty ('bounded rationality') may make it less costly, less risky or both to internalize inherently separate economic activities within the boundaries of the firm.

This internalization is held to be preferable to each such activity being undertaken by a separate economic agent. Costs to be avoided include those of drawing up separate contracts specifying precisely the rights and obligations of every party to every economic transaction. Risks to be avoided include those of opportunistic behaviour by counter-parties to an insufficiently specified contract and of failing to find a market for the output of functionally specialized ('idiosyncratic') investments.

Benefits of internalization resulting from reduced transaction costs and uncertainty may manifest themselves as variously:

- security of supplies and markets
- technical or engineering economies

- marketing economies
- financial economies
- managerial or administrative economies.

These will increase in importance with the frequency of transactions (Williamson, 1970).

The work of Coase and Williamson also assists in explaining the presence of organizational forms other than the firm. Williamson (1982) has developed the Coasean markets–hierarchy dichotomy to derive a more general theory of organizational form and to provide a foundation for the so-called 'transaction cost school' and some of the varied definitions of strategic alliances proposed and used in the literature.

In an area where theory, practice and analysis have been evolving so rapidly, definitional inconsistencies may reflect some more fundamental differences in approaches. Thus it is necessary to define a 'strategic alliance' as the term will be considered and used in this book.

A strategic alliance can be defined by reference to any combination of the following:

i)   the legal, structural or ownership *form* that the alliance takes
ii) the *nature* of the resulting relationship between partners through integration or interdependence
iii) the *purpose* of the relationship
iv) the *importance* of the relationship.

In addition, which complicates matters, each definitional criterion may be of asymmetric importance to some or all of the partners in an alliance.

i) Form
A strategic alliance is located on a continuum between, on the one hand, market based, arm's length transactions and relationships and, on the other, hierarchic, or intra-firm, transactions or relationships. The broad range of alliance types (see Figure 1.1) range from formal cooperative ventures through joint ventures and joint ownership to strategic investment in a partner.

A formal cooperative venture exists where two or more independent firms formally agree to work together for their mutual benefit. This agreement may be supported by a formal document (such as the

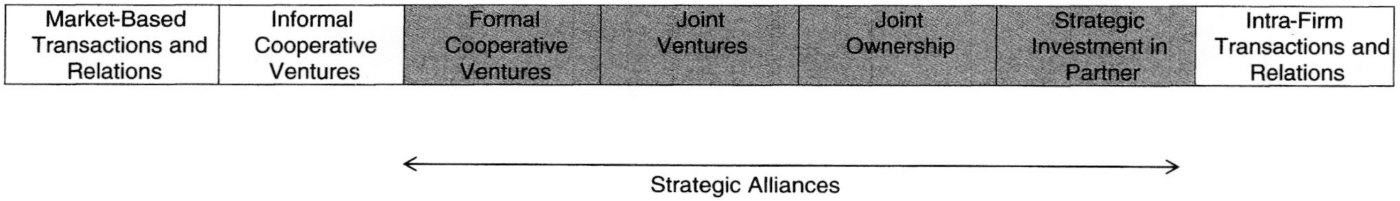

Market-Based Transactions and Relations	Informal Cooperative Ventures	Formal Cooperative Ventures	Joint Ventures	Joint Ownership	Strategic Investment in Partner	Intra-Firm Transactions and Relations

Strategic Alliances

Figure 1.1 Forms of Strategic Alliances
Source: Adapted and modified from Lorange and Roos (1992)

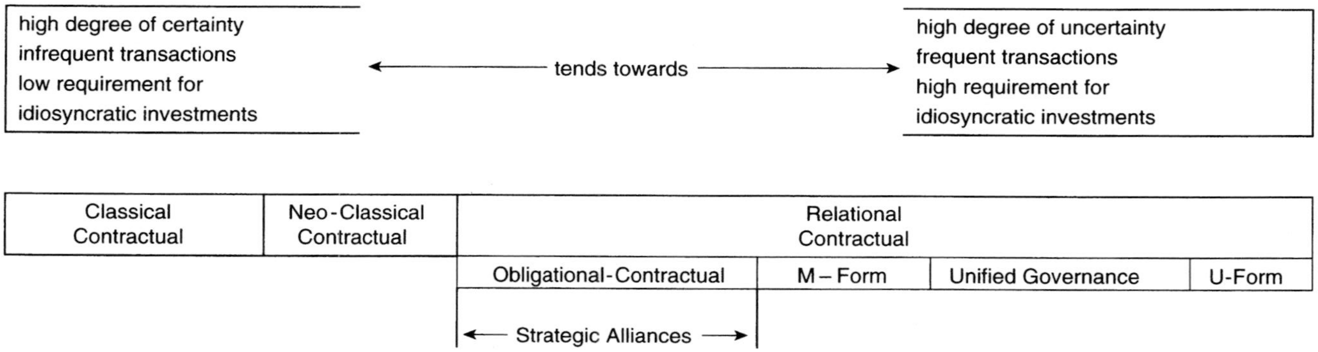

high degree of certainty
infrequent transactions
low requirement for
idiosyncratic investments

⸻ tends towards ⸻

high degree of uncertainty
frequent transactions
high requirement for
idiosyncratic investments

Classical Contractual	Neo-Classical Contractual	Relational Contractual		
		Obligational-Contractual	Unified Governance	
		M – Form		U-Form

Strategic Alliances

Figure 1.2 Nature of Strategic Alliances
Source: Adapted from Williamson (1986)

17 page BNP-Dresdner Cooperation Agreement) or perhaps by little more than an oral agreement between the respective chairmen.

A joint venture is a separate company in which all the founding firms have an equity stake. A joint venture is usually governed by its own board of directors.

Joint ownership arises where two or more independent firms jointly own an asset, such as a manufacturing or bottling plant, to serve the interests of the owning firms.

A strategic investment in a partner typically involves one firm in taking a small investment in another to support their agreement to work together. This often takes the form of a share-swap, as a gesture of mutual commitment rather than as a precursor to a merger or to exploit formal ownership rights.

ii) Nature

A strategic alliance is a sub-set of the relational-contractual part of the markets-hierarchy continuum (see Figure 1.2) and more especially the obligational-contractual part of that continuum. Firms that know each other, and have worked together or entered into one-off contracts in the past, can be deemed to have a pre-existing 'relationship' by virtue of having freely entered into new contracts. This is termed a relational-contractual arrangement. By entering into strategic alliances, firms go a crucial stage further by obligating themselves to enter into future contacts and transactions with their alliance partners. This is termed an obligational-contractual arrangement.

iii) Purpose

A strategic alliance represents an attempt to strike an optimal balance between the conflicting needs and purposes of economic activity, as outlined in Figure 1.3. It seeks to balance the various benefits to be received from collaboration against the external and internal forces that may push the alliance in the direction of evolution (to a full merger, say) or to dissolution.

iv) Importance

Another way of classifying alliances is to differentiate between 'non-strategic' and 'strategic' alliances. The 'strategic' alliance is typically one which displays high levels of resource commitment, is (or is expected to be) of long or open-ended duration and whose purposes represent a core activity of a strategic nature for one or more of the partners. Figure 1.4 summarizes this differentiation.

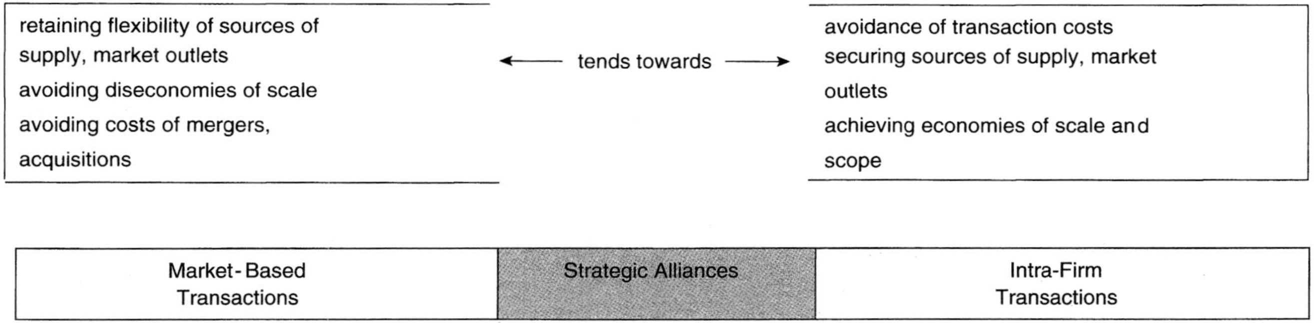

7

Figure 1.3 Purpose of Strategic Alliances
Source: Adapted from Glaister and Buckley (1994)

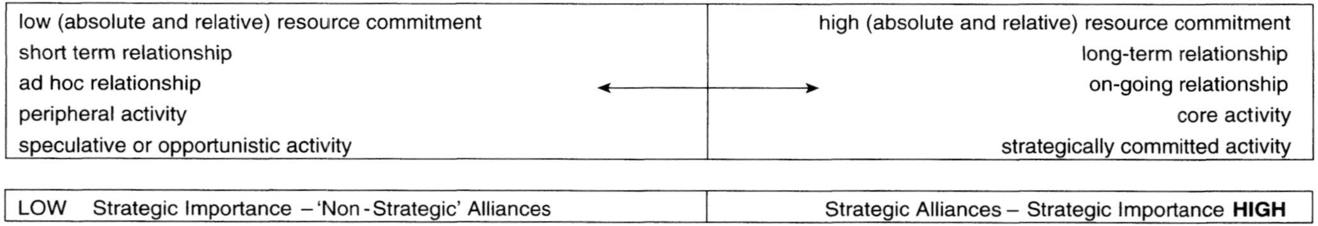

Figure 1.4 Importance of Strategic Alliances
Source: Adapted from ul-Haq *et al* (1996)

From the above analysis we can derive a general definition of a strategic alliance as proposed by ul-Haq *et al*, (1996) thus:

> A durable relationship established between two or more independent firms, involving the sharing or pooling of resources to create a mechanism (corporate or otherwise) for undertaking a business activity or activities of strategic importance to one or more of the partners for their mutual economic advantage.

Strategic alliances – a taxonomy

Faulkner (1995) expands the work of Lorange and Roos (1992) and Williamson (1986) by classifying strategic alliances on three dimensions, which he defines as the scope of the alliance, the legal status of the alliance and the number of partners in the strategic alliance.

In the case of the scope of the alliance, Faulkner differentiates between Focussed [F] and Complex [C]. Focussed Scope refers 'to a collaborative arrangement between two or more companies, set up to meet a clearly defined set of circumstances in a particular way' (Faulkner, 1995). Complex Scope refers to cooperation over a wide range of areas either as whole organizations or various parts of organizations.

In the case of the legal status of the alliance, Faulkner differentiates between the Joint Venture [JV], which requires the creation of a separate company, and the Non-Joint Venture [NJV], which has flexible and fluid boundaries. He also describes the NJV as a collaboration which may range from limited to broad in its scope and is most appropriate when the 'extent of the possible relationship is impossible to foresee at the outset'.

In the case of the number of partners, Faulkner differentiates between Two Partners [2] or More Than Two Partners [>2]. He also calls the latter 'a consortium'. Faulkner's classification system complements this analysis by expanding the number of axes to include the scope of the alliance.

Alliances could be focussed on a pre-defined set of objectives (for example, the transfer of specific knowledge from one firm to another) or a complex set of objectives, where separate firms agree to cooperate over a diverse range of activities (or a range in between). An example of the former is the product-specific alliance between Royal Bank of Scotland and Scottish Widows and of the latter the geographically global and multi-dimensional alliance between Banque National de Paris (BNP) and Dresdner Bank. Table 1.2 above provides a comparison of these taxonomies.

Table 1.2   Comparison of Taxonomies

Lorange and Roos Classes	Faulkner Codes Focussed Scope	Faulkner Codes Complex Scope	Williamson Class
Formal Cooperative Venture	FNJV2 FNJV>2	CNJV2 CNJV>2	
Joint Venture	FJV2 FJV>2	CJV2 CJV>2	Obligational
Joint Ownership	FNJV2 FNJV>2	CNJV2 CNJV>2	Contractual
Strategic Investment in Partner	FNJV2 FNJV>2	CNJV2 CNJV>2	

Source: Lorange and Roos (1992); Faulkner (1995); Williamson (1986)

The strategic alliance versus the infrastructure alliance

The strategic alliance has, at its core, the characteristics proposed in the definition put forward by ul-Haq *et al* (1996):

i)   it has durability which may be of infinite duration;
ii) it involves the sharing or pooling of resources;
iii) it creates a mechanism–this may be a cooperation secretariat as at the core of the BNP-Dresdner strategic alliance or it may be a separate joint venture company as in the new, mainly Eastern European, overseas ventures in the same strategic alliance;
iv) it is of strategic importance to at least one of the partners; it may very well be of varied degrees of importance to the members of the strategic alliance;
v)   it is of mutual economic advantage, or more specifically confers a discernible competitive advantage to each of its members.

The infrastructure alliance, on the other hand, shares most of the characteristics of the strategic alliance (in particular items i–iv above) but differs in the crucial issue of item v). That is, the infrastructure alliance does confer a mutual economic advantage but does not confer a *differential* competitive advantage to its members.

These differences are examined below.

Strategic alliances

The strategic alliance is entered into to confer a competitive advantage to its members. Thus the 18th century goldsmith banker who had a good reputation and reciprocal obligational-contractual links with other goldsmiths could enjoy the economic return of lending via the issuance of notes and was thereby conferred a competitive advantage. Those goldsmiths who did not enjoy such obligational-contractual relationships could not benefit from this trade and suffered a competitive disadvantage in comparison to the former. An example of the former are the Medici or early Rothschilds, who had international obligational-contractual relationships and could achieve an economic benefit from participating in the letter of credit business and thereby enjoy a competitive advantage. Because these relationships were based on specific links made between goldsmiths and were of an obligational-contractural nature, we can therefore call them strategic alliances. Other *ad-hoc* links based on the general reputation of the goldsmith would be termed relational-contractural relationships and therefore not strategic alliances.

Being able to enter into these obligational-contractual relationships to access, variously, counterparties, fund transfer, credit and capabilities, confers a competitive advantage *in comparison* with those who were unable to enter into such relationships. These types of inter-bank relationships can be termed strategic alliances. Figure 1.5 summarizes this. The figure uses two axes – membership status and degree of competitive advantage conferred. A member of a strategic alliance will

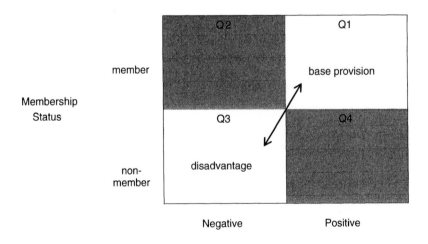

Figure 1.5 Strategic Alliances

only remain if membership provides a gain over non-membership. This rationale is shown in quadrant Q1. Non-members will be at a disadvantage, Q3, and will enter the alliance if there is some advantage to be gained by moving to Q1. The quadrants Q2 and Q4 are untenable. In the former a member will exit the alliance if there is a no competitive advantage to be gained from membership of the alliance, in the latter, a non-member cannot gain the advantages conferred by membership without being a member.

Infrastructure alliances

The infrastructure alliance is at the theoretical opposite end of the continuum from the strategic alliance. In its purest form it does confer a competitive advantage to its members, but membership is so broad that, in effect, all banks have access to its advantages and the infrastructure alliance acts as a basic foundation for the business being conducted by banks. This would mean that no one member of the industry would obtain a competitive advantage in comparison with another because all members of the industry would receive the same advantage, thus making it a 'base line provision'. Figure 1.6 below summarizes this analysis.

The figure uses two axes – membership status and degree of competitive advantage conferred. A member of an infrastructure alliance will remain because it provides a base line provision for its industry.

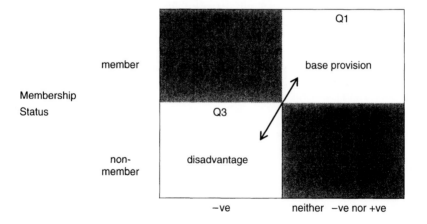

Figure 1.6   Infrastructure Alliances

This rationale is shown in quadrant Q1. Non-members will be at a disadvantage, Q3, and will be forced over time to enter the alliance to secure access to the same base line provision as its competitors provide unless it decides not to provide the services that this infrastructure alliance facilitates. The quadrants Q2 and Q4 are untenable so there is only a binary choice between Q1 or Q3.

To provide an example: Z-Bank decides to provide credit card services in the UK. To do so it will need to enter at least two infrastructure alliances, one to gain access to the payment systems that allow credit cards to be used in retail outlets, internet and telephone transaction – VISA or MASTERCARD, and another to gain access to the Automated Teller Machine (ATM) systems to allow cash withdrawals. For Z-Bank to not join these infrastructure alliances is to make the provision of credit card services impossible and would disadvantage them. However, membership has a neutral effect as competition in credit card services in the UK is based on price, additional services and products, for example, and no longer on ATM network provision. If Y-Bank does not wish to provide credit card services, then membership of the two infrastructure alliances discussed above is counterproductive because of the added cost with no benefit.

The above details the two extreme positions, on the one hand strategic alliances and on the other, infrastructure alliances. Neither position is considered to be an actuality. Most alliances probably lie on an intermediate position on a continuum with multiple choices co-existing and different opportunities being available.

The characteristics of the infrastructure alliance are complex and are examined in more detail below. The form of such an alliance may range along the continuum in Figure 1.1, and in particular it may be embedded within either a joint venture company or a network type relationship.

The strategic alliance was analyzed in Figure 1.2 in terms of three criteria after Williamson (1986):

i)   the degree of certainty
ii) the frequency of transactions
iii) the requirement for idiosyncratic investments.

On these criteria the infrastructure alliance differs greatly from a strategic alliance.

i) The degree of certainty
Infrastructure alliances typically provide a base line service that supports a day-to-day activity of the banking sector – for example, national or

international payment systems. Such systems require a high degree of certainty in a number of areas. Two examples are given below:

- the accuracy and reliability of the data transmitted to and from users of the system embedded in the infrastructure alliance and the ability to verify the identity of the transmitter and the recipient are critical;
- the robustness of the system in processing huge numbers of transactions over continuous periods with low error rates is essential.

These requirements lead to a need for clear operating parameters to be built into the design of the infrastructure alliance. The alliance has to operate according to those design parameters with change in the parameters only occurring occasionally and usually requiring some major event such as the establishment of the new venture to justify the change.

Payments systems require accurate, continuous, anticipatable and reliable operation. This can be characterized as a need for a high degree of certainty in the infrastructure alliance.

ii) The frequency of transactions

Infrastructure alliances such as payment systems are built on the requirement to process high volumes of transactions. These transactions may be generated by the increased globalization of trade in services and physical goods and the resulting need to transfer local and foreign currency internationally; by the increasing prevalence of bank accounts to receive salaries and direct debits and standing orders to pay bills; or by the increasing volume of foreign exchange, equities and funds traded domestically in the City of London or internationally in the global financial system.

This system-wide need for the processing of pre-identified frequent transactions is served by the infrastructure alliance.

iii) The requirement for idiosyncratic investments

Idiosyncratic investments are 'specialized human and physical assets [that] become more specialized to a single use, and are hence less transferable to other uses' (Williamson, 1982). Infrastructure alliances are generally intra-firm arrangements that are established to process specific transactions repeatedly in large volumes. The investments made – whether human capital, training, physical assets or machinery – are specific and specialized to particular transactions, they are idiosyncratic, and the requirement for such investments is high and economies of scale are forthcoming.

In summary, the infrastructure alliance requires a high degree of certainty in its scope, frequent transactions are the norm and a high requirement for idiosyncratic investments is displayed.

In modern Europe the majority of banks, even those that have a small and local scope, enjoy local and international relationships through direct membership of (or access through contracts with direct members of) infrastructure alliances such as:

CHAPS – The Clearing House Automated Payments System. This is a domestic UK based clearing system. It is a joint venture owned by a collection of banks, and all UK based banks can have access to its services through a contract with a member; the umbrella body is APACS.

SWIFT – The Society of Worldwide Interbank Funds Transfer. This is an international payments system which all banks may gain access to.

VISA and MASTERCARD – International payment systems that facilitate and underpin the use of credit cards.

ATMs – Automated Teller Machines. This is a cash notes issuance machine that is prevalent in large quantities in the domestic and international markets. Banks have access to other banks' ATMs either through an individual agreement or through membership of networks such as LINK.

EUROCLEAR and CEDEL – Other such infrastructure alliances exist in the clearing of bonds, equities and gilts, including the registration of ownership, and in a host of other areas.

These infrastructure alliances may originally have been strategic alliances that conferred a competitive advantage to the establishing members. One example of this is the strategic alliance between Royal Bank of Scotland and Banco Santander established in 1988. The partners developed a pan-European funds transfer system, IBOS, to provide a mechanism for the banks to deliver a service to their customers in small value European currency funds transfers. This placed 'two fairly small banks at the technological cutting edge of banking applications' (Faulkner, 1995). At the time of the establishment of IBOS, funds transfers of this type were made by sending bank drafts for collection. This was a time-consuming and costly procedure. By establishing IBOS, the Royal Bank of Scotland and Banco Santander were able to provide a cost effective and efficient service to their customers, a service that was not provided by other banks, and this conferred a competitive advantage to the member banks. Over time, IBOS became more international through establishing a New York link and allowed more members to join, thereby sharing the competitive advantage conferred by membership with more members. Eventually the membership is likely to be so broad that the service provided by the alliance may become a base line provision and the strategic alliance will become an infrastructure alliance.

An example of the broad membership of an infrastructure alliance is the Association of Payment Clearing Services, APACS, the umbrella body of the UK payments systems structure. Its operations consist of BACS (bulk electronic clearing for direct debits and credits), CCC (cheque and credit clearing), CHAPS and, since 1999, EURO CHAPS (same day electronic payments). Its total membership of 27 banks, from the USA, Australia, Germany, Holland, Japan and the UK affords 'remote access' to non member firms, in the case of EURO CHAPS, to over 35,000 sponsored users of BACS.

Current infrastructure alliances such as the ATM networks, now consisting of over 23,000 machines in the UK, generally provide access for all users. They tend to produce a 'level-playing-field' in this area of provision. If such service provision were restricted, increasing the barriers to entry, the regulatory authorities would doubtless step in to ensure access.

Indeed the infrastructure alliance is a core facilitator of banking activity. Without CHAPS, IBOS and SWIFT the transfer of funds would be more time intensive and cost prohibitive; without VISA and MASTERCARD the global credit card service would fail; without globally interlinked ATM Networks the multi-currency availability of cash on demand 24 hours per day service would fail. Infrastructure alliances are the foundation on which the provision of banking services is built. These are indicative of the pre-existing high propensity of banks to cooperate as discussed further in Chapter Two.

Nevertheless a bank may attempt to offer differentially priced access to a competitor in the financial services sector such as occurred in the Barclays-Nationwide dispute in 2000. Here Barclays attempted to impose an ATM access charge to Nationwide customers while not charging its own customers. Barclays' rationale was that it had invested heavily in its extensive ATM network for the benefit of its customers and to generate a competitive advantage. Nationwide had also invested in an ATM network, though both the network and associated investment were smaller. Barclays considered that higher charges to Nationwide customers were justified to balance out the unequal distribution and size of networks and to provide a competitive advantage to Barclays in recruiting and retaining customers. In 2004 the issue of oscillation from infrastructure to strategic alliance forms in ATM system provision came again to the fore.

It is not always clear, however, where the comparative advantage lies, and there is often an oscillation, along the continuum mentioned earlier, between the strategic and infrastructure alliance. Over time, the variety of service networks available and competition between providers will tend to drive prices to a temporally 'stable' point and reconvert this type of oscillating infrastructure alliance into an infrastructure alliance.

An established infrastructure alliance therefore usually generates a limited competitive advantage to its members. It may provide a short-term competitive advantage to members in comparison with entrants to the financial services industry who are not members, but these new entrants will also obtain access to this 'base line provision' and the position will move back into a stable 'dynamic disequilibrium'.

A bank can generate a long-term competitive advantage by establishing a new service as a start-up strategic alliance. This service, over a period of time, may confer an advantage to its members and a disadvantage to non-members. Eventually this service may become a base line provision, an infrastructure alliance. To give one example, Morgan Stanley was the primary founding member of the Euroclear equity clearing system and enjoyed the advantage of this strategic alliance with a small number of co-founding members. Now the system is taking on an infrastructure status, with Morgan Stanley and the other co-founders no longer enjoying a relative competitive advantage through being users of the Euroclear services but instead receiving a return on their investment as the equity owners of Euroclear.

Establishing a start-up strategic alliance of this technology-based type, perhaps destined later in its lifecycle to become an infrastructure alliance, leads to:

i) competitive advantage (in service provision and returns) in the short term;
ii) additional extraordinary (ownership) financial returns upon its conversion, in the longer term, to an infrastructure alliance.

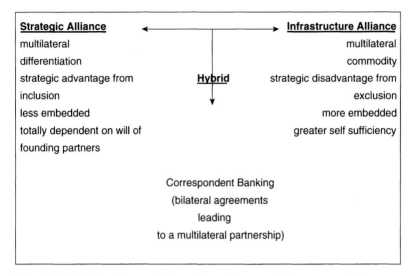

Figure 1.7   The Key Characteristics of Strategic versus Infrastructure Alliances

The key differences between strategic alliances and infrastructure alliances are displayed in Figure 1.7. The two forms are at the opposite ends of a continuum.

The strategic alliance is multilateral in membership; it provides a differentiated service that is only accessible to members; membership confers a strategic advantage to members and the alliance is less embedded in the nature of banking, rather it is a temporary choice to carry out a particular set of activities together. The strategic alliance governance and direction is dependent on the founding members.

The infrastructure alliance, on the other hand, enjoys a multilateral membership; it provides a service which is commodity like in its nature; it generates a strategic disadvantage to those excluded from membership; it is deeply embedded in the practice of banking and it is generally a separate form with its own managerial precepts, structure and direction.

The strategic alliance and infrastructure alliances are defined as opposite ends of the continuum. In practice a particular alliance will lean towards one or the other end in each characteristic and the balance position of the individual characteristics will determine if it is characterized as strategic or infrastructure. An example of this is correspondent bank relationships. These hybrid arrangements are made up by a set of bilateral agreements between individual banks that collectively establish a value network or multilateral partnership. Each individual bank may be a member of a number of value networks, which co-exist, and some provide the basis for later strategic alliances.

Conclusion

This chapter has introduced the core question being examined, detailed and reviewed the structure of this book and introduced its content. It has defined the subject of this book, the strategic alliance, and differentiated between the strategic alliance and the infrastructure alliance. Strategic and infrastructure alliances have been found to be important, but different, forms of business collaboration for banks and are necessary to facilitate their provision of services.

In this chapter the question 'Do strategic alliances add value?' has not been answered. Rather it is clear, at this point, that infrastructure alliances do add value to all the members through providing a 'base line provision' to enable banking activity.

Chapter Two examines how deeply embedded strategic alliances are in the banking sector and reviews the particular use of strategic alliances in Europe from 1960.

2
Industry Level – The Life Cycle of Strategic Alliances

Introduction

This chapter will identify and analyze the antecedents of the main forms of collaboration now prevalent in the European banking sector and use this analysis to develop a general theory of the lifecycle of strategic alliances in the European banking sector. To do this, the chapter will review the history of cooperation and determine the extent of the historical propensity of banks to cooperate. It will present a longitudinal analysis of the use of strategic alliances in three time periods: the 1970s, the 1980s and the early 1990s. The first time period will be analyzed in depth, the latter two more briefly. This analysis will delineate the mutually-influencing, co-evolving relationship between the formation and evolution of such alliances (the 'events') that have occurred over the periods and the links with broader changes in the economic, regulatory, business and banking environments over the same period (the 'mechanisms'). The terms 'events' and 'mechanisms' are as used by Lawson (1997), whose taxonomy is detailed in Appendix 1 of this book.

Finally this chapter will provide some observations regarding the lifecycle of strategic alliances in this sector and relate the findings back to the research question – Do strategic alliances add value?

The bankers' propensity to cooperate

Trade, that is the buying and selling of goods and services, is an integral part of daily life. The Phoenicians traded, or bartered, dyes and spices for tin obtained from Cornwall and the Scilly Isles. This trade required the existence of three primary factors: a double coincidence of wants, a mutually agreed measure of value and a store of wealth.

'A double coincidence of wants' refers to the need of both parties to the trade transaction to want to exchange what they have for what the other party in the proposed transaction has. If this coincidence subsists, then the parties to the trade transaction need to agree to the relative value of item one in terms of item two. These two conditions are sufficient in the case of the direct, and relatively immediate, trade of items such as one basket of fruit for two fresh fish. However, if the trade is not immediate then some items will also need to act as a store of value. Fruit and fish are perishable items, and as their value reduces over time a suitable non-perishable store of value needs to be found. This trading has been noted in all locations and has been conducted using a vast number of differing mediums of exchange and stores of value, including cowrie shells, sheep, cattle, knotted string and later metals such as bronze ingots. Copper was used in Rome, silver coins in Greece and iron in Ancient Britain.

The development of coinage, followed by paper notes and then international letters of credit is long and interesting. Only a few highlights will be mentioned here, as a prelude to contemporary cooperation among banking institutions.

Over time, gold and silver (the Persian silver-coin, the Abassi, for example) emerged as the preferred metals due to their longevity (they do not rust or rot) and the low bulk and high-ascribed-value combination. Thus gold and silver became generally acceptable in exchange for goods and services (Perry, 1981). Subsequently the gradual establishment of non-debasable coinage as the primary form of exchange took place.

To consider how these developments underpinned inter-bank relationships in Europe we take the English case. The use of notes developed in the seventeenth century from the deposit of gold and silver coin and bullion in the vaults and safes of goldsmiths and silversmiths and the issuance of ownership rights in the form of gold and silversmiths' notes over that physical bullion, which both receipted the deposit and promised to return the deposit on demand. Over time, the receipts or notes, rather than the underlying gold and silver, were exchanged for goods and services, with goldsmiths honouring the notes issued by other reputable goldsmiths. To facilitate trade these notes were later issued in fixed and easily tradable amounts and were made bearer-notes, payable to the holder. Accordingly gold and silversmith notes became easily exchangeable between traders of goods and services.

Goldsmiths' noting the tendency for substantial deposits to be left in the vaults and the requirement to generate a return from these static holdings led to goldsmiths 'lending' the property rights. This took place through the issuance of additional notes, for a finite period of time, to 'borrowers' who needed to finance their trading activities. Thus the gold and silversmiths acted as financial intermediaries, or bankers, between depositors and lenders in exchange for an acceptable return. These early bankers were involved in the business of 'offering services, such as the safekeeping and lending of money at interest' (Collins, 1995), and their involvement became an integral part of the activity of trade.

This borrowing and lending activity has, at its foundation, the need for strong reciprocal rights and obligations, and therefore a high degree of mutual trust. For example, the provision of coins to a trader by Goldsmith A against the presentation of a note issued by Goldsmith B requires Goldsmith A to believe that Goldsmith B will have sufficient resources and the will to honour its own note when presented for payment by Goldsmith A.

The general principles of financial intermediation discussed above are still evident. The goldsmiths' notes were eventually replaced by bank notes issued by The Bank of England against deposits of gold and silver. Banks thus took on the financial intermediation role between depositors and borrowers.

On the international side, goldsmiths' notes came to facilitate cross-border trade. A London based merchant would go to his banker, say Rothschilds, and request the issuance of a 'letter of credit' payable at Rothschilds' overseas branches and at its partner banks in other countries. The merchant would travel to, for example, Paris and approach the Rothschild branch or partner bank. At this branch or bank the merchant would draw funds against the letter of credit to pay for goods and services in Paris without carrying the risk of having gold or silver coin on his person. This international intermediation role developed into the issuance and negotiation of letters of credit, which – like the borrowing and lending activity described above – required the establishment of a strong reciprocal relationship with rights and obligations, and a high degree of trust, between banks in a number of countries.

This process was seen as early as the fourteenth century in continental Europe when, for example, the Medici bankers of Italy established international partnerships and branches to facilitate banking business. Lane (1985) notes that these international bankers 'needed large organizations to carry out their extended operations, and in order to mobilize the necessary capital, they developed forms of business organization that constitute a major contribution to the development of capitalism'. Prior to the 1340s these firms consisted of a head office with directly controlled branches overseas. In the post-1340s period, the Medici developed business structures that involved a head office holding company with subsidiary firms in the overseas locations. The international bankers utilized international bills of exchange to facilitate short-term borrowing and lending, and through this trade in bills created 'sophisticated money markets' (Lane, 1985). The development of European banking ranged through the areas of influence of the Florentine, Genoese, Tuscan, French, southern German and London bankers.

In order to carry out their functions of facilitating trade through the borrowing and lending of money nationally or internationally, bankers need to have a range of cooperative relationships with other bankers. This need for cooperative relationships is an *integral* and *essential* requirement to carry out the business of banking successfully. Bankers retain the right to choose with whom they establish cooperative relationships, and the configuration of these relationships, but the need to establish cooperative relationships is embedded in the nature of banking activity as detailed above.

The banker can, therefore, be said to have a high pre-existing general propensity to enter into cooperative relationships with other bankers, whether locally or internationally located, and these relationships are integral and essential to carrying out the business of banking.

This underlying general propensity to cooperate is seen in payment systems, in IT infrastructures and in money trade and exchange patterns. Infrastructure alliances, as discussed in chapter one, are at the core of banking and an example of the general propensity to cooperate; but this is not limited to multilateral networks. Indeed bilateral networks such as correspondent bank relationships (defined as 'agency relationships' where the agent is 'entrusted with the business of another' [Perry, 1979]) are usually built on relationship preferences. Banks do have a choice in determining the number, location and type of counterparties in correspondent bank relationships but generally not whether correspondent bank relationships are necessary to carry out their international business.

The next section will analyze more recent tangible forms of this general propensity to cooperate as seen during the 1970s through Club and Consortium Banks, during the 1980s through bankassurance, and during the early 1990s at the start of the use of virtual banks.

The use of strategic alliances in the European banking sector

The data sources and analysis methods

Three public sources of data were obtained and analyzed: *The Financial Times World Banking* special edition, published annually; *The Economist Survey of International Banking,* published annually; and the *Bank of England Quarterly Bulletin* section on *Developments in International Banking and Capital Markets.* These documents were obtained from 1970 for the 23-year period ending December 1993.

This chapter reviews the 'mechanisms' and 'events' that occurred over the period. Mechanisms are, according to Lawson (1997), 'structured things...that possess causal powers which, when triggered or released, act as generative mechanisms to determine the actual phenomena of the world'. Mechanisms are the changes in the underlying economy, regulation, technology and so on that lead to new observed opportunities, the 'events' that are within the 'actual domain of reality' (Lawson, 1997). These events may include, for example, increased competition, more demanding consumers, the opening up of cross-border activities (such as a result of the European Union). The terms are as used by Lawson and are discussed in Appendix 1.

The analysis determines and identifies the close interrelationship between the mechanisms and changes in mechanisms and the occurrences and changes in the events.

The broad analysis method was to:

i)   identify the broad changes in the economic, regulatory, business and banking environments (the mechanisms) over the period that underpin the events identified below;

ii) identify the concrete strategic alliance events mentioned in the data sources; the data sources are the primarily annual (quarterly in the case of the Bank of England) reviews of trends in the banking sector; a mention in these data sources was considered to be reflective of the perceived high importance of the event in the sector and over the time period. Over the period under review this method would allow one to track the major events in the sector;

iii) establish the relationship between these trends in observed events and the trends in changes in the underlying environments.

The 1970s – the era of Clubs and Consortium Banks

Changes in mechanisms in the 1970s

In the post-war period there has been a global trend towards dismantling the pre-war and wartime controls that reduced freedom of choice and movement in capital and current account transactions. This liberalization of capital movements was successful in facilitating a substantial and unprecedented growth in international trade. One important stage in this liberalization trend was the establishment of Euromarkets.

Euromarkets were established, primarily in London, in the 1960s. The term 'Eurocurrency' refers to 'deposits of [convertible] currency...which are held by people who do not live in the country whose currency it is, and who keep the deposits in a third country' (Perry, 1979). The primary London Eurocurrency was US dollar funds held by non-USA nationals in banks based in London.

The foundations of the Euromarkets, based on the interchange of funds between banks (and later corporations), were laid down in a number of economic and political events in the 1960s.

First, the USA had levied a withholding tax on interest and dividends remitted abroad to residents outside the USA on their holdings of investments. The US dollar had by this time become, post Gold Standard, the international reserve currency, and the demand for dollars by international investors, institutions and governments was high. The effect of this tax was to increase the propensity for foreign investors to deposit their US dollar holdings outside the USA.

Second, both UK and US authorities restricted overseas lending by their home country banks, thereby curtailing the ability of these banks to increase their exposure to foreign risk through the existing channels.

Third, the imposition of Regulation Q (for internal economic management purposes) in the US put a ceiling on interest rates that could be paid on deposits held in the US. The position of the US dollar as the international reserve currency led to the need for external agents to hold US dollars, while Regulation Q capped the return on those holdings. Investors therefore sought locations outside the USA to place their US dollar deposits, locations where interest rates would be fully subject to the interplay of supply and demand. Given its established, strong and innovative financial services sector, London provided such a location. This type of mechanism also occurred when Switzerland banned interest on Swiss franc deposits held in Switzerland by non-resident holders and led to the transfer of Swiss Franc currency holdings to London.

Fourth, the USSR had a requirement to hold assets in the reserve currency to meet its external liabilities. However, the Cuban Missile Crisis confrontation between the USA and the USSR in 1962 raised concerns in the Soviet Union that its US dollar holdings in the USA could be sequestered or frozen by the USA government. The London based Moscow Narodny Bank was instructed to place US dollar deposits in non-USA banks located in London. The Moscow Narodny Bank was majority owned by and acted as the overseas arm of the Central Bank of Russia and would have a contractual relationship with the London based bank. The London based bank would be subject to supervision by the Bank of England (and its home country Central Bank) but would operate in London under UK laws and regulations. Thus the USA government would not have the power to sequester or freeze USSR owned funds held in London without application to and the agreement of the UK judiciary.

These were the major factors that started the establishment of the Eurocurrency market, and its growth and development were substantial, integral and price sensitive:

Substantial – By 1966 this market accounted for about US$10 000 million in deposits. By 1972 this figure had risen to over US$82 000 million (*The Economist*, 1973) of which the US dollar accounted for about 80 per cent of transactions and balances.

Integral – The Eurocurrency market is closely linked to the changes in national polices and international sentiment and is an integral part of global fundraising for governments and corporations.

Price Sensitive – This market facilitates the cross-border flow of funds in accordance with changes in interest rate differentials or the pressures of speculation.

Euromarkets (deposits, bonds, equities) extend beyond the physical boundaries of Europe and constitute an international money and capital market accessible to all participants. They are not subject to any form of central regulation. Euromarkets facilitated the flow of funds from countries that were in surplus to those countries that were in deficit and became an essential element in the international trade mechanism. This function is clearly seen in the OPEC-led oil price increase in 1974 and the subsequent recycling of surplus.

The Organization of Oil Producing and Exporting Countries (OPEC)

In 1974 OPEC, a price cartel established by the major oil producing and exporting countries, increased the price of crude oil four-fold. This sudden increase in the price of raw material providing much of the energy requirements of the world had major effects on Euromarkets and the nature of the relationships between bankers and sovereign debtors. In addition to the more general economic effects there were four specific effects of the oil price increase.

i)   OPEC members generated substantial surplus funds.
ii) Developed countries faced a decrease in surplus funds.
iii) Developing countries faced a lack of funds to meet core oil based energy requirements.
iv) The bankers' role in 'petrodollar' recycling came to the fore.

OPEC members, primarily based in the Middle East, received a substantial increase in funds from the oil purchasers. These funds were initially denominated in US dollars, as global sales of oil were and are denominated in US dollars per barrel. The OPEC countries placed these funds on deposit in banks, with a substantial portion placed in the London Eurodollar markets. Due to the, largely Arab, depositors putting a premium on liquidity, these deposits were mainly placed at the short-term end of the spectrum. This meant that depositors could withdraw their funds at short notice, although in most cases, at least in the early days of this deposit boom, funds were rolled over and, in effect, became medium-term deposits. The increase in funds in the Euromoney markets from this source was high and led to high liabilities and the need to find remunerating assets to balance the bankers' books.

The developed countries were, and remain, the major global consumers of oil. The OPEC oil price increase led to a large increase in their energy costs. In the main, developed countries had relatively strong domestic economies and associated credit ratings so that they could increase their borrowings on the international markets. Thus developed countries faced higher energy bills, which were paid for by increased borrowing on Euromarkets, including the issuance of Eurobonds.

The non-OPEC developing countries were also dependent on oil, both to carry out their ongoing activities and to provide power to enhance the movement away from agriculture and commodity raw material dependence towards appropriate industrialization. In general, developing countries did not have credit ratings to borrow on the Euromarkets on the same terms as developed countries.

Bankers were receiving massive increases in their short-term liabilities through the deposit of petrodollars and were forced to seek asset investment opportunities. These would be required to generate a sufficient return to pay the interest cost of the deposits and operating costs, and profit needs, of the banks. In addition, the international agencies such as the IMF and the World Bank, along with developed country governments, were seeking global solutions to the requirement to recycle petrodollars to often less creditworthy borrowers (in this scenario, the developing countries). Some recycling through international agencies and government aid took place, but many plans for international public sector solutions to the issue of recycling petrodollars to non-OPEC developing countries were proposed, tabled, discussed but not enacted. Pressures on bankers, both from shareholders to find sufficiently remunerating assets to offset growing OPEC deposit based liabilities and from the international community to recycle petrodollars, led to sovereign borrowers being targeted. Commercial borrowers, though accessing the Euromarkets, were not sufficiently large to soak up these enormous surpluses. Developing countries had substantial funding needs to pay for their oil imports, and bankers eventually flocked to lend to them.

Short-term funds received from OPEC-based depositors were lent on a long-term basis to developing countries directly to public (and private sector) borrowers. The generally held premise was that national governments would not default on their debts. Bankers accordingly carried out their intermediation roles and converted short-term deposits to long-term loans. This process simultaneously boosted the size of Euromarkets and their importance in the structure of global financial flows. International Bankers had put themselves in the peculiar position of holding extra-long term assets in the form of loans whose principal, it would transpire, would not be re-paid by sovereign borrowers whose treasuries raised substantial funds through deposits sourced from the wholesale Euromarkets. This position led to the increasing need to continue to develop a global capital market larger than any one national location could support, and the need to draw smaller national, domestic banks into the provision of surplus funds to the wholesale Euromarkets, thereby ensuring the supply of funds.

The internationalization of trade and banking

The policies, or changes in mechanisms, underlying the generation of a global capital market, as discussed above, were underpinned by postwar economic policy moves towards free trade and substantial growth in the international trade in goods and services.

International trade activity by multinational firms requires financing in the form of letters of credit, bills of exchange and loans to build, for example, local and overseas manufacturing capacity. In addition, governments need to borrow to build the infrastructure to support these activities. Euromarkets provided the only source of funds of the size required to meet the scale of operations of multinational firms.

Bankers follow, rather than lead, income streams generated by meeting the financing needs of business activity. Manufacturing and trading form the basis for internationalization, and bankers internationalize in order to service their multinational corporate clients' requirements; bankers establish operations in countries where their multinational customers establish operations. As the Bank of England noted: 'The expansion of international business has been accompanied by the development of world-wide banking networks, on a more sophisticated level then hitherto, to ensure that financial services are available to meet the needs of the biggest international companies.' (*Bank of England Quarterly Bulletin*, 1973).

This parallel drive towards the internationalization of banking can be carried out in a number of ways:

i)   a mobilization strategy,
ii)   an 'own branches' strategy,
iii) a club (loose consortium) strategy,
iv)   a consortium bank strategy.

i)   The *mobilization* strategy has at its core the view that what is critical is the capital or funds that a bank has access to or can mobilize, rather that the amounts it wields. London merchant banks hold this view. In the purest form they are not in themselves providers of funds but can mobilize substantial funds, on a transaction by transaction basis, through their contacts and relationships.

ii)   The *own branches* strategy is one where the bank believes that relationships with other banks, through club or consortium banks, are fraught with managerial difficulties and that such difficulties are substantially larger than the benefits provided. Followers of the own branch strategy would prefer to establish their own wholly owned branches, representative offices and subsidiaries in overseas countries, thereby controlling their own international network. The major USA banks that followed their corporate clients overseas by establishing their own networks preferred this strategy.

iii) The *club* strategy is often a development from existing correspondent relationships (see Chapter One for a discussion of the Infrastructure

Alliance – Strategic Alliance dichotomy). Here a set of banks which may know each other through these correspondent links agree to work together without setting up a separate joint venture company or under-taking a cross-shareholding. A statement of intent is often sufficient to initiate the collaboration.

iv)   The *consortium bank* strategy involves a diverse group of banks subscribing fresh capital to a newly formed joint venture company, the consortium bank. This approach enjoys elements of the mobilization and own branches strategies.

   The foregoing has considered the changes in the macro-environment, the 'mechanisms' that underpin the development of new opportunities for the banks. The following subsection analyzes the growth, develop-ment and decline of clubs and consortium banks, the observed 'events' that result from the change in opportunities discussed above and makes explicit the life cycle of such organizational arrangements.

Clubs and consortium banks

In 1964 Midland Bank entered into a club arrangement called Midland and International, based in London, with the Standard Bank of the UK, Commercial Bank of Australia and the (Canadian) Toronto-Dominion Bank. Midland bank was a leader in the adoption of this strategy. It:

i)   started earlier in using strategic alliances to internationalize,
ii)   finished later and still uses some element of alliances,
iii) learnt through strong cooperation,
iv)   had relationships with major correspondent banks that under-pinned the alliances.

This club arrangement heralded the start of a trend to internationalize by establishing club and consortium banks that lasted into the 1970s. During this period the dominant change in the structure of banking practice was the increasing involvement of many older established banks, of various nationalities, in clubs and consortium banks. They offered merchant and/or commercial banking services in a multitude of international locations. The major banks were clearly divided between those that considered the club or consortium bank model the way forward and those that did not. This subsection will concentrate on the former.

   The *clubs* consisted of two or more banks that agreed to work together *without* formalizing this agreement as a separate legal entity. Lorange and Roos (1992) would code these arrangements as 'Formal Cooperative Ventures' (as discussed in Chapter One), and Faulkner would code them as 'FNJV>2', a focussed non-joint venture alliance of more that two partners, or 'CNJV>2', a complex non-joint venture of more than two partners. In Faulkner's (1995) pantheon, 'focused' refers to an alliance 'set up to meet a clearly defined set of circumstances in a particular way' with 'clear remits and understanding of respective contributions and rewards' while 'complex' is where members of the alliance 'recognize that, in combination, they form a potentially much more powerful competitive enterprise than they do individually, and while they are willing to co-operate with each other over a wide range of activities, they nevertheless wish to retain their separate identities and overall aspirations'.

The *consortium bank* model would be coded by Lorange and Roos as 'joint ventures' (that is, a separate legal form with various [usually more than two] shareholders and its own board of directors) and by Faulkner as a 'FJV>2', focussed joint-venture with more than two partners, or 'CJV>2', complex joint-venture of more than two partners, or more broadly a consortium.

The majority of clubs and consortium banks were set up in the late 1960s, with some earlier established groups such as Midland and International in 1964 and laggards such as the Orion group in 1970.

Table 2.1 provides an analysis of the geographical scope of partners of the clubs and consortium banks. The table analyzes 18 club and consortium banks (Cs and CBs) set up during the period 1964 to 1970 as reported in *The Economist* (1970). After this report a number of changes occurred in the composition of Cs and CBs, with additions and deletions of members and associated changes in geographical scope. For purposes of this analysis, the position as at November 1970 is considered and the findings used to provide insights into this phenomenon.

A number of observations can be made:

i)   the date of establishment of the Cs and CBs,
ii) the location of the Cs and CBs,
iii) the purpose of the Cs and CBs,
iv) the membership spread of the Cs and CBs.

i)   The *date of establishment* reflects the timing of willingness to use cooperative solutions to the growing internationalization needs in the case of member banks. This underlying propensity to enter into Cs and CBs is over and above the general propensity to enter into cooperative relationships displayed in all banks, as discussed above. Midland Bank

Table 2.1   An Analysis of the Geographical Scope of Clubs and Consortium Banks

	Name	Base	UK	USA/Canada	Far East	France	Germany	Italy	Belgium	Holland	Switzerland	Scandinavia	Corporate
1	Midland and International	London, 1964	Midland, Standard	•	•								
2	Banque Europeenne de Credit a Moyen Terme	Brussels, 1967	Midland Samuel Montegue			•	•	•	•	•			
3	International Commercial	London, 1967	National Westminster	•	•		•						
4	Societe Financiere Europeenne	Paris and Luxembourg 1967	Barclays	•		•	•	•		•			
5	European-American Banking Corporation	New York, 1968	Midland				•		•	•			
6	Intercontinental Banking Services	London, 1968 Lloyds and Bolsa, Chartered	Lloyds, Barclays			•							

Table 2.1 An Analysis of the Geographical Scope of Clubs and Consortium Banks – *continued*

	Name	Base	UK	USA/Canada	Far East	France	Germany	Italy	Belgium	Holland	Switzerland	Scandinavia	Corporate
7	Western American	London, 1968	Hambros	•••				•		•			
8	Atlantic International	London, 1969	Charterhouse, Japhet and Thomasson	••••		•		•					
9	Banque Occidentale	Paris, 1969		••		•							
10	Manufacturers Hanover Ltd	London, 1969	N.M. Rothschild	•				•					
11	Rothschild Intercontinental	London, 1969	N.M. Rothschild	•••		•		•	•	•	•		
12	Scandinavian Bank Ltd	London, 1969										•••••	
13	London Multinational	London, 1970	Barings	••							•		
14	United International	London, 1970	Williams and Glyns	••		••	•	•		•			
15	European Bank's International Company (EBIC)	London, 1970	Midland				•		•	•			

Table 2.1   An Analysis of the Geographical Scope of Clubs and Consortium Banks – *continued*

Name	Base	UK	USA/Canada	Far East	France	Germany	Italy	Belgium	Holland	Switzerland	Scandinavia	Corporate
16 Orion Banking Group	London, 1970	National Westminster Bank	••			•						
17 Euro-Pacific Finance	Melbourne, 1970+	Midland		Fuji-Japan								
18 Berne's Bank for Investment and Credit	Switzerland, 1970+									•		••

Key: Each entry = 1 member bank

Source: The Economist (1970)

entered into the Midland and International Club in 1964 (item 1), predating the Banque Européene de Credit à Moyen Terme (item 2), of which it is also a member, by three years. Midland Bank was therefore an early adopter of the club concept. This was based on its existing strong correspondent relationships used to facilitate international transactions. Midland is seen again as a member of four other Cs and CBs (items 2, 5, 15, 17), which would reflect its judgement that Cs and CBs deliver strategic advantages and tangible results. On the other hand, Williams and Glyns waited until the Cs and CBs concept was well established and only entered into the pan-European United International arrangement in 1970.

ii)   The *preferred location* of Cs or CBs is in London, with 12 of the 18 analyzed based there. One is based in New York (item 5), one in Australia (item 17) and four in other European locations: Brussels (item 2), Paris and Luxembourg (item 4), Paris (item 9), Switzerland (item 18). All but one of those not based in London have a London based member. This and the preferred location reflects the predominance of London at the centre of Euromarkets, the source of much of the funding provided to the multinationals whose internationalization the Cs and CBs sought to serve.

iii)   The *purpose* of Cs and CBs is, in the main, to provide international banking services, leasing and advisory services on an international basis to (multinational) clients. In addition, Cs and CBs allow access to the Euromarkets for those banks that do not have an independent presence in London (for example Scandinavian Bank Ltd [item 12]).

To take a hypothetical example: A UK based corporation may be expanding its operations into continental Europe and the USA. In the UK it can access funds through its local primary bank and make separate business arrangements with banks in, for example, France, Belgium, Holland, Switzerland, the USA and Canada. The UK banker, seeing this trend and wanting to both retain the UK relationship and capture part of the income stream of the overseas activity may enter into a C or CB arrangement. Thus the Rothschild Intercontinental arrangement has member banks that are present in all the countries mentioned above. The C and CB would assist customers thereby providing an international service without each member undertaking the heavy capital investment and additional risk of setting up dedicated branches overseas. In addition, the group would have a greater capacity to access Euromarkets for funds.

iv)   The *membership spread* of the Cs and CBs as detailed in Table 2.1 shows a concentration on North America and Continental

Europe, which would reflect the sources of major expansion of multinational business and trade in this era. The USA banks' involvement is not fully representative of the USA banking sector. The major money centre (largely New York located) USA banks preferred to establish their own wholly owned overseas branches or representative offices and displayed skepticism towards the benefits of the Cs and CBs concept. The more regionally and domestically concentrated USA banks, such as National Bank of Detroit and First Pennsylvania Banking and Trust Co., entered into Cs and CBs as an access point to the Euromarkets.

Within this general spread, individual Cs and CBs have particular foci. To take the example of the varied Cs and CBs of which Midland Bank is a member: Midland and International (item 1) builds links between the UK, North America and the Far East; Banque Européene de Credit à Moyen Terme (item 2) is solidly continental European; European-American Banking Corporation (item 5) is based in New York to access the New York markets and links with the UK and three continental European countries; EBIC (item 15) is continental European; and Euro-Pacific Finance (item 17) is based in Melbourne to service the Far East *from* the Far East.

Whilst most C and CBs were alliances of banks, The Berne Bank for Investment and Credit (item 18) was established using a new idea, including major multinational firms as members of the C and CB for the first time.

This membership or geographical spread can be categorized as:

i)   same country Cs and CBs,
ii) geographically focussed Cs and CBs, and
iii) geographically diffuse Cs and CBs.

i)   *Same country* Cs and CBs are established to provide member banks with a greater presence and capacity to borrow and lend. An example is the Scandinavian Banking Partners Ltd (item 12) an alliance with members from a number of Scandinavian countries.
ii) *Geographically focussed* Cs and CBs concentrate on carrying out banking activity in a particular region or location in the world. An example of this is the Euro-Pacific Finance (item 17) concentrating on the Far East.
iii) *Geographically diffuse* Cs and CBs have members or shareholders from a number of centres. They are not focussed on carrying out banking business in a particular geographical location but rather wish to

capture the benefits of increased transaction size and risk sharing. An example of this is the United International (item 14) cross-European and North America Cs and CB.

The lifecycle of clubs and consortium banks

The post Second World War period was characterized by an increased liberalization of controls on capital and current account transactions. This process was successful in facilitating a substantial, and unprecedented, increase in international trade. Part of this change was the growth in the mobility of capital. During the 1960s a number of restrictive actions by governments – the USA imposing a withholding tax on US dollars, the USA and UK restricting overseas lending by their home banks, the USA Regulation Q capping interest rates paid on deposits and the USSR requiring to hold the international reserve currency (the US dollar) outside USA control – led to increased deposits in London based banks. These Euromoney deposits (broadly defined as currency held in a country where the held currency is not the home currency) started the development of the Euromarkets, centred on London. This rapidly growing Euromarket soon became the preferred source of funds for syndicated loans to companies expanding overseas to enjoy the benefits of liberalization in trade, particularly in the 1960s to 1970s periods. In 1974 OPEC (The Organization of Oil Producing Companies) increased the price of crude oil four-fold. This action resulted in OPEC members generating substantial funds; developed countries facing a decrease in surplus funds and developing countries facing a lack of funds to carry through oil based energy requirements.

Substantial deposits of 'petrodollars' now boosted the size of the Euromarkets. Failed public sector initiatives to recycle the petrodollars from OPEC to developing countries led to a core role in recycling for the Euromoney bankers, with a substantial increase in lending to sovereign and overseas corporate borrowers.

The internationalization of trade led to the need for companies to source banking services overseas. Additionally governments required funds to develop infrastructure to support increased trade and further funds to provide, now increasingly expensive, oil based energy requirements. Euromarket bankers followed these income streams by meeting the financing needs of manufacturing and trading that form the basis for internationalization. The bankers internationalized in order to service their multinational corporate clients' requirements and established operations in countries where their multinational customers established operations.

Expansion by bankers would take three forms – a mobilization strategy (mobilizing funds on a contract by contract basis through their contacts and relationships); an own branches strategy (establishing one's own operations overseas); a club or loose consortium strategy (through establishing strategic alliances with other banks). The choice of form is dependent on the degree of perceived certainty of the income stream that the banker is following. An own branches strategy requires a high commitment of capital, increased risk, full returns and more difficult exit. The Cs and CBs strategy requires a low commitment of capital, reduced risk, shared return and easy exit.

All Cs and CBs are a response to an opportunity or threat resulting from a change in the macro-environment, a change in the underlying 'mechanisms'. Opportunities develop as changes in the market take place and the development of the European Union is a major factor. 'Looking ahead, we in the Bank have been giving thought to the changes and problems in the banking world which we may expect to come as the nine nations of the Community progress along the road to economic and monetary union. In particular it seemed to us that the British banking industry might see advantage in some changes in structure in order to more effectively compete in the wider market for banking services now opening up' (*Bank of England Quarterly Bulletin*, 1973).

This opening up of the European banking sector led to the identification by, for example, Z-Bank directors of an opportunity to provide banking services to multinational customers in a third country. Z-Bank could realize this opportunity through a number of methods. It could merge with or acquire another bank in the overseas country; it could grow its own operations in the overseas location through varied degrees of involvement (for example a representative office [with marketing responsibility, transactions booked at home location] or a branch [marketing, management and transaction booking in the overseas location]); or it could enter into an alliance. Z-Bank directors would choose the appropriate method of realizing the potential gains, and mitigating the potential losses, of a macro-change, and the method used would vary as the conditions changed. The Cs and CBs strategy could be the first step into a new market place. As the market developed and Z-Bank gained more confidence in the continuation of the income stream, the bank could invest more resources in the operation, for example, setting up its own representative office or branch or merging with or acquiring an overseas partner. The Cs and CBs approach could be the appropriate method of entering into a new geographical, product or service market but the rationale could change over time and alternative methods could be utilized.

As noted earlier, the establishment of Cs and CBs started in 1964 with the Midland and International grouping. A further three were established in 1967 and three more in 1968. In 1969 and 1970 the trend reached its zenith, with five and six Cs and CBs established. Thereafter the establishment of Cs and CBs was reduced. Scrutiny by the EEC of possible anti-competitive effects of Cs and CBs may have reduced the potential validity of this collaborative strategy. By 1974 very substantial growth in the activities and importance of the Euromarkets provided a stronger case for UK and continental European banks to change their internationalization strategy to an own branches and representative offices rather than a Cs and CBs strategy. The UK and continental European bankers used the Cs and CBs strategy only as long as it was viable. When the business case changed and potential regulatory constraints were perceived, these bankers made pragmatic decisions to move away from the cooperative to the solo approach.

Amongst the banks that entered into Cs and CBs there were a range of adoption rates – at the extremes early and late adopters. Midland Bank was an early-adopter of this strategy, commencing its first club arrangement in 1964. A late adopter Orion Group, by comparison, did not enter until 1970. Here Clubs are classified as banks that agree to work together without formalizing this agreement as a separate legal entity whilst a Consortium Bank has a joint venture structure.

The analysis of 18 Cs and CBs in Table 2.1 is undertaken by reference to the date of establishment, the location, its purpose and its membership spread. The date of establishment was an indicator of propensity of particular banks to enter collaborative arrangements. Early adopters had a higher propensity, late adopters a lower propensity. The preferred location was London for 12 of the sample. The remainder whilst headquartered overseas all but one had London based members probably reflecting the London's position at the heart of the Euromarkets, the source of much of the funding that the Cs and CBs sought to provide to multinationals. This purpose was expanded with the addition of leasing, international banking and advisory services. The membership spread, mainly in North America, UK and Continental Europe, reflects the major expansion of multinational business and trade in this era.

Within this group of 18 Cs and CBs the geographical spread is of interest. Same country groupings allow an enhanced presence and capacity, geographically focussed groupings concentrate their activities

Table 2.2   Origins of Cs and CBs Participants

Country/Region of Origin	No. of Participations
North America	22
UK	20
France	8
Germany	7
Holland	7
Scandinavia	6
Italy	5
Belgium	4
Far East	4
Switzerland	3
Corporates	2

Source: Extracted from Table 2.1 Geographical Location of Members of Clubs and Consortium Banks.

in a particular region and geographically diffuse groupings' core driver is to enable increased transaction size and risk sharing.

Table 2.2 shows 64 occurrences, as reported in The Economist, 1970, of UK and continental European banks belonging to Cs and CBs. These were the major banks in their country. In the UK all four major banks, Midland, Lloyds, Barclays and National Westminster, were involved in Cs and CBs with a total of 16 continental European banks, which are also, in the main, the major banks in their home country. The EEC feared that this would reduce cross-European competition with its attendant drawbacks.

The original rationale for the Cs and CBs, to internationalize rapidly while minimizing the risk and costs of establishing strong international relations and accessing the expertise of the partners, was undermined by the increasing business rationale for an 'own branches strategy'.

In addition increasing regulatory attention and concern as to the anti-competitive potential of Cs and CBs also contributed to a declining rate of establishment of Cs and CBs arrangements. The growing importance of Cs and CBs to the City of London was recognized by the

40

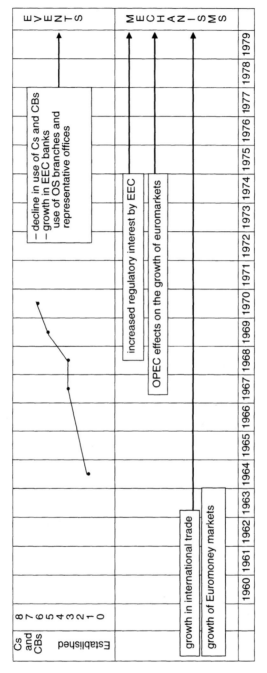

Figure 2.1 The Rate of Establishment of Clubs and Consortium Banks, 1963–1970

Bank of England Quarterly Bulletin Statistical Annex inserting a new category of banks, 'Consortium Banks', in the 1976 Bulletin (*Bank of England Quarterly Bulletin*, 1976) that did not exist in the 1975 Bulletin (*Bank of England Quarterly Bulletin*, 1975). Over time as the rationale for Cs and CBs changed existing Cs and CBs were run down, resulting in residual elements remaining intact or continued as vehicles for a future trans-national merger (Scandinavian Banking Partners [item 12] being eventually liquidated in 1997) or bought out by a partner bank and turned into a merchant banking flagship (Orion).

The relationship between changes in 'mechanisms' (the Euromoney markets, OPEC, internationalization, regulatory interest) and changes in 'events' (the growth and decline of C and CB arrangements) is broadly summarized in Figure 2.1.

The 1980s: The era of Bankassurance

The previous section has reviewed in detail the growth and decline, the lifecycle, of Cs and CBs in the banking sector. Two further life cycles of strategic alliances in the UK banking sector can be identified: the growth of Bankassurance and the increased use of Virtual Banks. The purpose of the rest of the analysis in this chapter is to briefly review the events leading to the development of these collaborations and to draw attention to the continuation of these trends, and not to provide a comprehensive analysis.

UK banks were in a unique position to adopt a Bankassurance strategy. Whilst in the USA a legal separation of commercial banking and investment banking activity has been in force ever since the Glass-Steagall Act of 1933, the Universal Bank model held sway in Germany and Switzerland. The USA position was based on the reportedly mistaken belief that the banks' activities in the securities markets caused the Wall Street Crash of 1929 and subsequent economic depression. The alternative Universal Bank model combined the major activities of intermediation of banking and insurance in both the retail and wholesale sectors with the securities market roles of investment management, securities issuance, distribution and trading.

In the UK the traditional segregation between merchant banks and commercial banks was still largely prevalent, with each operating in its own markets. This segregation was based on established practice rather than diktat. In the 1980s, however, this segregation began to break down, with commercial banks growing their own merchant banking operations (for example, County Bank, a subsidiary of

National Westminster Bank). Alongside this gradual blurring of distinctions between commercial and merchant banks came the abolition of single capacity stockjobbers (a middleman between client and stockbroker) and stockbrokers (traders in stocks and shares) in favour of dual capacity firms in the securities sector. Restrictions on foreign ownership of UK institutions and securities were also relaxed.

During 1983 to 1985 these changes resulted in thirty commercial banks based in London (of which 14 were of foreign origin) purchasing 26 stockjobbers, nine stockbrokers, 10 merchant banks and one insurance company (*The Economist*, 1985). This was a major drive towards consolidating ownership of financial institutions in the hands of commercial banks, thereby forming Universal Bank style organizations that encompassed commercial, investment and merchant banking activities.

The broad movement in London's securities sector was towards securities firms being acquired by capital rich commercial banks. These commercial banks also faced pressures of increased competition that drove up the cost of funds from retail depositors and drove down yields in corporate lending and securities transactions. In addition, the Bank for International Settlement's Capital Adequacy Accords increased both the need for more capital and the cost of capital. This led to a further need to increase the yield on the funds employed. The retail sector was focussed on as the sector that would allow banks to generate the required high returns because it was characterized by a substantial number of transactions of relatively low individual transaction value.

The high volume retail sector had high associated transaction costs. IT based solutions to basic processing needs were effective in increasing the efficiency, decreasing cost per transaction and thereby increasing the gross yield per transaction.

During the mid-1980s the nature of individual customers was also changing to information-rich customers who were more discerning and value-for-money conscious and who could, at low cost, switch from one service provider to another. Counterbalancing this was the increasing demand per household for a number of different financial services needs and the banks attempting to establish multi-product relationships with their customers.

Such relationships were based on a current account with the cross selling of credit (overdraft, loans, mortgages), savings (accounts, endowments, annuities), securities (purchase and sale of equities, asset management), travel services (travellers cheques) and so on. Two areas missing in the banks' product range were life assurance and general insurance. This type of product required new skills, and the banks purchased these skills by entering into strategic alliances with assurance and insurance companies (these alliances came to be termed 'bankassurance'). The alliance usually required the assurance or insurance company to provide processing, actuarial and pricing skills while the bank acted as a distributor of products to its customers. Providing assurance and insurance products on this basis also made limited calls on bank capital, as the liabilities of contracts were covered by the amalgamated premiums under management and not the underlying institutional capital. The aggregate trend was towards the rapid establishment of a number of alliances between banks and assurance and insurance companies with the subsequent merger of some alliances if the business case warranted it. Unlike the club and consortium banks, decline of Bankassurance arrangements is not nearly so rapid, with such arrangements broadly categorized at the maturity stage of the lifecycle as displayed in Figure 2.6.

The 1990s: The era of the Virtual Bank

The previous sections have identified two lifecycles of strategic alliances, of Cs and CBs and Bankassurance strategies, in the UK. The lifecycles are built on the existing high propensity of banks to enter into cooperative arrangements to facilitate their business as discussed earlier in the 'The Bankers' Propensity to Cooperate' section. As the business case for these alliances grew the number of alliances grew and vice versa. In the case of the Cs and CBs lifecycle a decline is identified whilst with the Bankassurance lifecycle a maturity phase is posited.

The nature and lifecycle of Virtual Banks is qualitatively different to both the Cs and CBs and Bankassurance configurations and lifecycles. The purpose of the remainder of this chapter is to examine this assertion further.

The traditional view of firms, as exemplified by Coase (1937) is that firms are independent organizations with discernible boundaries. They choose to work with other firms as the business case warrants it but essentially this collaboration is still between two discernible firms, unless they give this up through a merger or acquisition or through establishing another firm, a joint venture. In more recent strategy literature Porter exemplifies this approach in the Value Chain (Porter, 1985, 1988) and the Value System (Porter, 1985).

44

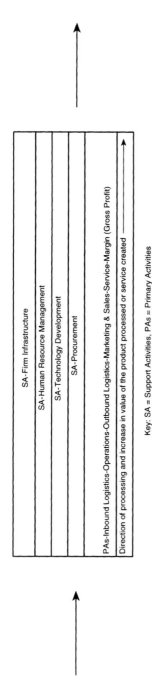

Key: SA = Support Activities, PAs = Primary Activities

Figure 2.2   An Individual Firm's Value Chain, adapted from Porter (1985, 1988)

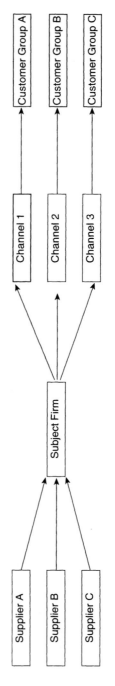

Key: Arrow = Implicit or Explicit Contracts, Box = Individual Firm or Group

Figure 2.3   The Value System and Linkages, adapted from Porter (1985, 1988)

The organization's *Value Chain*, Figure 2.2, identifies a firm as having within its boundaries (often in terms of both corporate control and physical location) all the operational functions – inbound logistics, operations, outbound logistics, marketing and sales, service – progressing the raw material from inbound logistics through the operations cycle, each of which adds value to the product (for example). The achieved sale price minus the cost of operations and activities that support the firm's operations of the firm – firm infrastructure, human resource management, technology development and procurement – is the achieved margin, the operating profit of the firm. This model, at its very basic, has two core conditions – that all activities of the firm are carried out within the firm and that the production process is typically on one site. Whilst the second condition does not always hold, the first generally does. The model is primarily based on a linear manufacturing process and does not take into account the simultaneous production and consumption nature of services.

The *Value System*, Figure 2.3, links the organization's value chain with the organizational value chain of three other parties or firms – suppliers, distribution channels and the customer. Porter's argument was that competition was no longer between individual firms but between the value system of one firm as compared to the value system of another firm. Further the quality of one value system is dependent firstly on the quality of the member firms and secondly on the quality of linkages between them.

Johnson and Scholes (2002) take this further, asserting that 'as organizations build e-commerce relationships within the value system there may be shifts in 'architecture' of the value system towards a value network'. They define a *Value Network* as a 'value system where the inter-organizational relationships are more fluid'.

In the case of alliances in the banking sector, as discussed above in 'The Bankers' Propensity to Cooperate', there is a general existing propensity to collaborate. There is also a high specific propensity to collaborate at the business level to provide the infrastructure to facilitate transactions and to access knowledge, processing power, to gain access to products, markets and customers. This specific propensity has been documented earlier in this chapter through the analysis of Cs and CBs and Bankassurance relationships.

These alliances are part of a continuum ranging from the early obligational-contractural relationships of Goldsmiths, through a general propensity to collaborate in correspondent bank and infrastructure links, to the specific propensity to collaborate displayed in the two lifecycles already analyzed.

The key difference in the virtual bank lifecycle, as compared with Cs and CBs and Bankassurance lifecycles, is the enormous power of the supporting technology, now available to all, to underpin and facilitate increasingly complex value systems and networks. The computer technology (email, data transfer, low cost telecommunications, virtual groups, seamless integration are a few examples) is now invasive and prevalent in most industries.

This technology allows one to build a virtual value system where the physical co-location is not so important. A services firm such as a bank can now locate its headquarters in London and its call centre in India. It can link to its suppliers via electronic procurement systems and to its customers via the internet and email.

The capabilities of technology have been revolutionary in disaggregating the Coase (1937) conception of a firm. In his view the firm is a locus of intent and control with clear boundaries between the firm and the rest of the world in which the firm operates. Porter's value chain sums up this view and his value system shows the linkages between, mostly, independent firms (value chains) to build up a process from supplier to the customer. The technology allows the firm to situate its value system in many locations, linked electronically, and employ techniques such as just-in-time supply, overseas call centres, electronic ordering and third party delivery. The revolution is in the possibility of dismembering the firm's own value chain. The firm can outsource elements of its previously main activities – human resources can be run by Hays, IT by IBM, physical production in China by a third party firm and marketing via an agency in New York – with the 'firm' retaining headquarters, strategy, finance and contracting in London.

By and large the Coasian firm of clear and closed boundaries no longer exists as far as co-location is concerned, though not as far as ultimate control of the firm's strategic intent, in the developed world. Instead the firm may be defined as the imposition of a strategic intent over a number of activities, many carried out in different physical locations and by third party providers. The firm is now perceived as a bundle of, largely explicit and some implicit, contracts. The facilitator of this approach is information technology.

This approach allows the bank to decide which activities to carry out, which activities to outsource and even which part of the firms value chain to consider as its core activity. This latter decision would be based on the individual competencies of employees and the aggregate capability of the firm.

According to Johnson and Scholes (2002), information technology changes the nature of competition by changing the nature of the industry. A generic example is that barriers to entry can be raised due to the upfront investment, incumbents are still tied to previous links and at the same time barriers are lowered due to better informed and less loyal customers; the power of suppliers increases because of the possibilities for forward integration; buyers become more knowledgeable and therefore more discerning and demanding; substitutes increase both through different delivery channels, providers and alternative products and hyper-competition increases with markets becoming more commodity-like with rapid replication of new ideas.

In retail banking in the UK, the blurring of distinctions between banks and non-banks, in relation to strategic alliances, came to the fore in the 1990s when the entry of non-bank providers of financial services into the UK retail sector was marked. Organizations with a strong brand name with the retail consumer (Marks and Spencers, Sainsburys, Tesco, Virgin) set up, variously, banking operations providing retail services such as credit cards, savings, mortgages, personal loans, life assurance and general insurance. These services were dependent on strategic alliances with bank, life assurance and general insurance companies to provide the products and services fronted by and sold through retailers.

For example, the primary alliances of Tesco Personal Finance Limited are with The Royal Bank of Scotland, Scottish Widows and UK Insurance. The Royal Bank of Scotland provides banking expertise, including credit scoring, the management of assets and liabilities, the collection of regular payments, and the issuance of credit cards; Scottish Widows provides life assurance policy processing and management skills; UK Insurance provide, for example, motor insurance. Products are branded under the Tesco Personal Finance name and marketed through Tesco shopping sites, website and direct mail.

Sainsburys Bank is an equity joint venture between HOBS (Halifax Bank of Scotland) and the retailer, Sainsbury plc. The value network encompasses over 90 strategic or infrastructure alliances that together allow Sainsburys Bank to deliver retail financial services in the UK. The Core Value Network is outlined in Figure 2.4. It shows the clear linkages between the primary parties and details how each operation in Sainsburys Bank has a link with a corresponding (in terms of action rather than title) part of HOBS and Sainsburys plc. It is these many linkages that are the strength and enablers of the alliance.

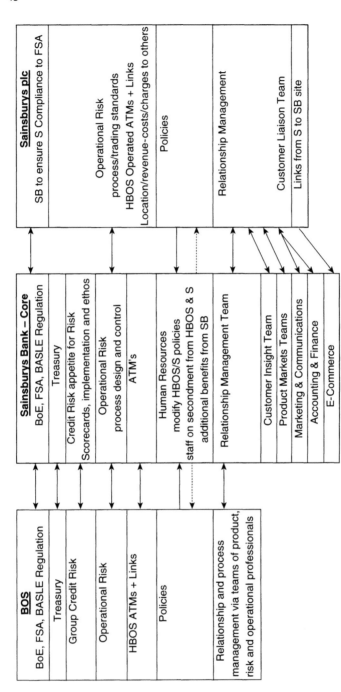

Figure 2.4 The Core Value Network of Sainsburys Bank
Source: D. Bottom, Deputy CEO, Sainsburys Bank (2002). Total Network = 90 + Strategic Alliances
Note: HBOS = Halifax Bank of Scotland, SB = Sainsbury Bank (Joint Venture type Strategic Alliance between HOBS and S), S = Sainsbury plc

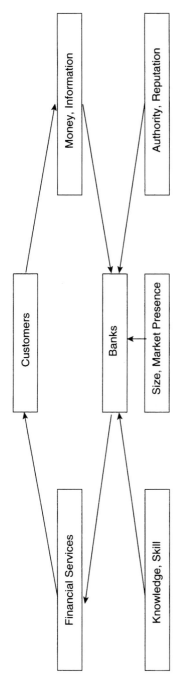

Figure 2.5   The Value Loop
Source: Morison (1999)

The foregoing has detailed how the Coaseian conception of the firm has changed, yet, by and large, the supply of raw materials and the consumption of the products and services is still carried out by different parties. In banking this is not the case. Morison (1999) details the assets of financial institutions as:

i)   information ('about customers and markets'),
ii) skill ('in using that information to assess, price and monitor risk'),
iii) good reputation ('for probity and professionalism'),
iv) authority ('to undertake deposit-taking and other core business activity'),
v)   size ('to generate economies of scale and scope...in particular to spread risks widely'),
vi) customer base ('and a delivery system for reaching and serving those customers').

Inputs into a bank – money and information – are provided by the same customers who consume the services of a bank. Morison posits the *Value Loop* (Figure 2.5) in which 'banks add value to the money and information they received from their customers by deploying their key attributes of skill, size, reputation and market presence'

Discussion and conclusion

This chapter has analyzed the history of cooperation in the banking sector with a focus on the relationship between changes in the economic, regulatory, business and banking environments and the establishment and evolution of strategic alliances.

As a result of this desk research a number of observations can be made:

First – Bankers have a high pre-existing propensity to enter into cooperative relationships with other bankers, whether locally or internationally located. The commercial need for a base level of such relationships (for example, correspondent banking links) is deeply embedded in the very nature of banking.

Second – The choice of whether to enter into higher-level strategic alliances is one that is dependent on the strength of the business case. If the potential income stream is initially insufficient (either in size or security) to justify full-scale investment, the strategic alliance allows the firm to share cost, risk and returns while testing the business area prior to this investment. The strategic alliance is a discernible event, embedded in changes in mechanisms, in the context, in which the strategic alliance partners operate, and involves a deliberate choice to enter into an alliance instead of some other route. The strategic alliance will last only as long as the business case justifies this rather than an alternative strategy.

Third – The alliance entry process is one where changes in the context within which the bank or banks operate lead to *potential* new business income streams. Bankers then make decisions as to whether to service this potential income stream and which strategy to employ. If they decide to follow the income stream using a strategic alliances based approach, then pragmatic decisions need to be made on the partners, form, scope and so on of the resulting alliance.

Fourth – Once a strategic alliance is entered into, its longevity depends on its success in generating returns for its partners as well as the continuation of the business case for such an alliance. The Cs and CBs alliances of the 1960–1970s displayed a short lifecycle because the business case for a solo strategy became so strong. The bankassurance alliances of the 1980s still generate sufficient returns for partners to continue their collaboration. Over time, the nature, scope and form of alliances co-evolve with the context in which they operate.

Fifth – The development of new technology has changed the nature of Coase's (1937) conception of a firm of clear and closed boundaries, which by and large, no longer exists in the developed world. Instead the firm may be defined as the imposition of a strategic intent over a number of activities, many carried out in different physical locations and by third party providers. The firm is now perceived as a bundle of, largely explicit and some implicit, contracts. The facilitator of this approach is information technology. This approach allows the bank, or non-bank financial services provider, to decide which activities to carry out, which to outsource and even to decide which part of the firm's value chain to consider as its core activity. This latter decision would be based on the competencies of its individual employees and the aggregate capability of the firm. In the specific case of a non-bank financial services provider, the concentration would be on marketing and branding with the production side outsourced to other specialist providers.

Sixth – The lifecycle of a strategic alliance can vary both with the steepness of growth and decline sections of the curve and the duration of the maturity plateau. In Cs and CBs strategic alliances the growth curve was steep, the duration of the maturity plateau short, and the decline curve steep. In bankassurance strategic alliances the growth curve was steep, the

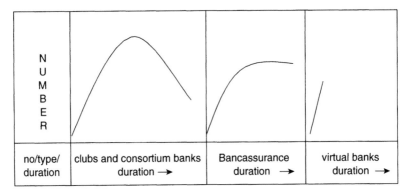

Figure 2.6 The Lifecycle of Strategic Alliances, 1963–1999

duration of the maturity plateau long and the decline, except at the margins, yet to come. In Virtual Bank strategic alliances the growth curve is still steep and will continue because information technology has changed the nature of the marketplace. This is summarized in Figure 2.6.

What insight does the foregoing analysis provide into the research question – Do strategic alliances add value?

Clearly at the level of the European banking industry the infrastructure alliance is very important to underpin and enable activities and bankers display a high propensity to use such alliances. Strategic alliances, on the other hand, were traditionally more dependent on a decision that new business streams are most appropriately captured by this mechanism. In the case of both the 'Clubs and Consortium Banks' and 'Bankassurance' strategic alliances lifecycles the bankers made a specific decision to use a strategic alliance approach, for what turned out to be a finite time.

So, infrastructure alliances add value. Strategic alliances are more complex. They are entered into if it is considered that they would add value and dissolved when they have not, or an alternative approach would add more value. The current virtual bank lifecycle is not the same as the previous lifecycles. Technology has now changed – fundamentally – the bank's ability to use focussed strategic alliances to outsource and relocate parts of the firm. Strategic alliances may be used whenever and for whatever function and time that they add value, and not used if they do not. The period of time between use and non-use is greatly shortened.

The next chapter considers the foundations of strategy, major perspectives used in the analysis of strategic alliances and provides a review of key academic papers published on the subject.

3
Strategic Alliances – The Theory and the Literature

Introduction

This chapter provides a review of foundations of strategy, major perspectives used in analyzing strategic alliances and a summary of key academic papers. The review details a number of theoretical perspectives – economic (market power, transaction cost, agency, increasing returns, game), strategic management and organization (population ecology, resource-dependency, organization structure and management, organizational learning, trust) – and adds to understanding the lifecycle of a strategic alliance in the commercial world, from stages of formation through management and evolution to dissolution.

Strategy

Pettigrew, Thomas and Whittington (2002) refer to primary concerns of the strategist as addressing questions about the 'purposes, directions, choices, changes, governance, organization and performance of institutions in their industry, market and social, economic and political contexts'. Concerns of the strategy practitioner and strategy researcher are, by necessity, broad, holistic, complex and action orientated whilst also focussing on the specific, to inquire in depth, to reduce complexity to manageable proportions through frameworks, models and matrices, to provide insights for reflection and prescriptions for practice.

These counterpoised trends lead to development of two primary threads in the strategy field: first, practitioners who make decisions in, for example, market contexts and, second, strategy academics researching in firms but through a lens of their own research contexts and traditions. The practitioner uses preferred tools, methodologies and perspectives to carry out analysis and make decisions; the academic works within research traditions be they qualitative or quantitative, positivist or idealist, primary or secondary. Both practitioners and scholars are affected by national and industry context or, in the latter case, by traditions of the academic subject or institution. An ongoing dialogue between scholars, between practitioners (managers, consultants) and between scholars and practitioners leads to evolution of the strategy field.

Strategy scholars operate in research and discipline traditions that presuppose particular preoccupations. The scholar, aside from engaging with the practitioner world, engages with other scholarly disciplines, borrowing from and contributing to them. Accordingly, it is necessary to review the development of strategy in the academic literature prior to considering the literature on strategic alliances.

Strategy, as a scholarly discipline, is generally considered to have commenced in the early 1960s with Chandler's (1962) development of the dictum that structure follows strategy and work on rationalism and planning championed by Ansoff (1965). Schendal and Hatten (1972) proposed a more economics based, analytical, positivistic and quantitative approach to strategy whilst Porter (1980, 1985) continued this industrial economics based emphasis and language into the scholarship and practice of strategy. With this the focus became the structure of the industry rather than the nature of the firm. The sub-disciplines of this approach include market power, transaction cost economics (commencing with Coase, 1937), agency, increasing-return theory and game theory. Whipp (1996) argued that the single discipline, industrial economics approach to strategy was flawed, that strategy was an important field and required cross-boundary fertilization of ideas.

Hoskisson *et al* (1999) reviewed the practice of strategy scholarship and saw a concentration on examination of factors that affect performance of the firm. They further saw a to-and-fro movement of the 'pendulum' from internal (the firm, internal context) to external (the industry, external context), principally: 1960s and 1970s (business policy – internal); 1980s (industrial organization economics – external); mid-1980s (organizational economics – internal/external); 1990s (resource and knowledge based – internal). Alongside this swing in internal-external orientation were also, according to Hitt *et al* (1998), swings in the level at which analysis took place, theoretical orientation and research methods utilized. Thus industrial organization economics based work and its derivatives use analysis of surveys and databases, while internally based researchers' core interest is in obtaining and using tangible and intangible (knowledge) resources and requires smaller sample studies via case or survey methods.

The field of strategic management is still largely dependent on the industrial organizational economics view, that is, based on rational external industry analysis and positioning the firm in an appropriate place in its market/s, an intended strategy approach. Alternative views are expounded by writers such as Mintzberg *et al* (1976) who pondered the nature of the processes internal to the firm by which strategic decisions were formulated. Mintzberg characterized this process as one of an 'emergent strategy' where the 'emergent' (bottom up) and 'intended' (top down) strategies would combine to form a third 'realized' strategy different, but drawing, from its two constituent parts.

Managerial and research practice in strategy is subject to preferences. That is, emerging management techniques are justified through their perception as a sound means of achieving outcomes that are important and an improvement upon previous techniques. These 'fads and fashions' (Abrahamson, 1996) shape the behaviour of managers, leading to positive or negative impacts on firms, employees and customers.

Whipp (1996) writes about his concern for the lack of reflexivity in the relatively new strategic management field, perhaps due to the multiple stakeholders (scholars, executives and consultants) having differing agendas and working according to differing timescales and levels and types of analysis.

The industrial organization economics approach, made popular by Porter, has a strong hold on practice through MBA syllabi and its application directly in firms and through consultancies. Bourgeois (1984) was an early commentator on the flaws of this deterministic school and drew attention to the:

i)   reductionist nature,
ii) lack of examination of causal links between structure of the industry and behaviour of the firm,
iii) lack of study of content and process of strategy reciprocally and simultaneously,
iv) lack of combination of qualitative and quantitative data use,
v)   lack of appreciation of the need to move from industry level context to the firm level context.

Future development of strategy has at its core the change towards a greater link between the external world within which the firm operates and the internal world of the firm. Decades ago, but in a work still influential, Coase in 'The Nature of the Firm' (1937) defined a firm as an organization that 'consists of the system or relationships which come into existence when the direction of resources is dependent on an entrepreneur'. He asserted that business activity is carried out either in 'free' markets or within boundaries of a firm and that by organizing and co-ordinating resources, capabilities and directing production the 'manager-entrepreneur' in a firm can gain a significant cost advantage over market based transaction costs.

How then does the manager-entrepreneur access these resources? Mergers and acquisitions allow control but do not easily allow integration; organic growth is costly and takes time; and co-opting another firm's resources is both less costly and allows short-term access. The manager-entrepreneur no longer requires total ownership of resources but rather the ability to 'rent', and control resources as necessary. Accordingly, the primary concern is to be able to gain access to, configure and manage these resources, wherever located, to meet the firm's needs.

This approach opens up the firm's boundaries, making them permeable to other firms (but still within the control of the rent paying firm) to include co-opted resources. Collaboration with other firms becomes the norm. As Burton (1995a) writes, strategists need to take a 'Composite Strategy' approach and:

i)   choose the combination of competitive and collaborative strategies that are appropriate in the various dimensions of the firm's industry environment
ii) blend the two elements together so that they interact in a mutually consistent and reinforcing, and not counter-productive, manner; so as to
iii) optimize the firm's overall position, drawing upon the foundation and utilization of both collaborative and competitive advantage.

In this scenario the Porter model of competitive advantage is supplemented by the Burton model entitled 'The Five Sources Framework'. In this framework (as displayed in Figure 3.1) determinants of collaborative advantage are analyzed and (together with determinants of competitive advantage) are appropriately and co-reinforcingly mixed to provide a Composite Strategy. A core decision is whom to ally with, which webs of firms to collaborate with and what role to play in those webs.

As Pettigrew, Thomas and Whittington (2002) state, 'A combination of highly porous firm boundaries, denser information links, pervasive

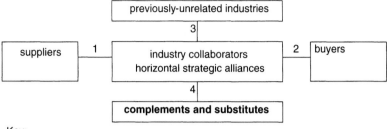

Key:

1. relational contracting and quasi-integration with suppliers
2. partnering with channels/buyers
3. prospecting diversification alliances
4. related diversification alliances

Figure 3.1   Analyzing Collaboration: The Five Sources Framework
Source: Adapted from Burton (1995a)

issues of trust and reciprocity and the constant imperative to find, retain and motivate talent make the interface between strategizing and organizing a constant challenge'. Strategy is no longer one side of a dichotomy of strategy and implementation. Rather it is an active and interlinked process of strategizing and organizing for advantage in comparison with competing firms and webs, the latter made up of multiple strategic alliances of firms.

Strategic alliances are obligational-contractural relationships that are in-between markets and hierarchies. They are not free market competition or internalization with one firm rather an agreement to work together, in certain areas, for mutual benefit. They require member firms to agree to collaborate, to share resources, to allow the 'rent' of capabilities, tangible resources and distribution networks for a period of time that suits the member firms. The volatility of markets and industries that the firms and strategic alliances operate in ensures that such alliances only last as long as they confer a collaborative advantage.

The key perspectives

Scholars use and promote a number of perspectives to discuss strategic alliances and joint ventures. Each perspective provides insights into the theory and practice of strategic alliances but, by itself, is not sufficient to view the full complexity of alliance activity.

The perspectives can be said to fall into broad groups of Economic, Strategy and Organization.

Economic perspective

The output minus input relationship is here under scrutiny. An organization may wish to increase its dominance of a market and therefore the ability to charge extraordinary rents. Alternatively, it may wish to build trust endowed relationships with alliance partners to minimize costs and maximize potential payoffs.

Market power theory

Market power or monopoly theory, has at its core the concept of dominance, of high barriers to entry and therefore reduced potential competition. The higher the market share or monopoly/ quasi-monopoly enjoyed by the firm, the higher the barriers to entry of potential competitors, the greater the autonomy in setting high prices and thereby the ability to increase profits. Strategic alliances may be used in a negative sense to provide a forum for collusion between participants in the same industry or they may be used in a legitimate form to, for example, secure and develop know-how.

In this perspective, offensive coalitions diminish the competitors' market share or increase their production and distribution costs while defensive coalitions build increased barriers to entry, thereby attempting to secure the position of alliance member firms by reducing competition and increasing profits.

The 'value chain' concept, introduced by Porter (1985) can be used to distinguish between:

i) alliances that seek to provide increased economies of scope, reduce risk by sharing, including knowledge. Here the intention is to increase market share and secure economies of scope, a cost leadership strategy,

ii) alliances that link different parts of the value chain of the partners to the alliance in a complementary way so as to enhance their overall competitive advantage, a differentiation strategy.

Market power theory allows for both methods in generating enhanced market power and therefore increased returns. In this approach, strategic alliances are an alternative choice, alongside competitive or acquisitional strategies for increasing this power, and participants make a continual, and opportunistic, choice between cooperative or competitive alternatives.

This theory assumes that industrial, national and international contexts – the structure of markets, regulation and so on – will determine and constrain the appropriate strategy. It therefore does not give much credence or importance to how member firms may use an alliance proactively.

Transaction cost economics theory

Transaction cost economics is grounded in the work of Coase (1937), wherein the boundaries of the firm are examined. Firms are established because the entrepreneur-manager can manage the organization of resources in a more effective and cost optimizing way than the marketplace. By reducing costs, the entrepreneur may realize the opportunity to reduce prices (and compete on the basis of price) while retaining the same margin, or to maintain prices (and compete on a differentiation basis) while increasing the margin enjoyed. Firms expand as the manager-entrepreneur takes more transactions under his or her control, and firms shrink as their ability to manage the higher volume of transactions, in comparison to the market mechanism, decreases. Williamson (1985) noted that 'a transaction occurs when a good or service is transferred across a technologically separable interface'. Transaction costs are incurred as a result of negotiation costs, drawing up contracts, logistics and monitoring. They reflect costs incurred in 'arranging, managing and monitoring transactions across markets' (Child and Faulkner, 1998).

The stark choice provided by this perspective seems to be either to carry out economic transactions through market-based exchanges or to internalize them within a single firm. However, Williamson (1986) argues that multiparty, reoccurring transactions will take place when:

i)   the choice of partners is limited,
ii) market conditions are complex and/or uncertain,
iii) there is information asymmetry,

and that the governance structure to be used should be based on attributes of the transaction to be undertaken (asset specificity). That is, one-off, relatively short-term duration, non-specific asset based transactions are suited to market based mechanisms ('Markets'). Where transactions are recurrent, have uncertain outcomes with long lead times and require unique or transaction-specific investments, they can be more effectively conducted within firms ('Hierarchies').

Williamson proposes that two further possibilities lie between these extremes depending on the frequency of transactions.

i)   if occasional frequency: market based contracting supported by third party arbitration and litigation is the appropriate form of governance

ii) if of reoccurring frequency: relational contracting (long-term investment in building relationships between members) and bilateral governance (mutual investment of specific assets that generate mutual dependence and act as hostages against opportunism) are more appropriate. These latter factors admit the possibility of intermediary (between markets and hierarchies) forms of organization such as obligational-contractural relations including strategic alliances.

This theory is primarily concerned with a static point efficiency and discloses little about development of trust in relationships, a matter which is discussed later in the chapter. A detailed analysis of strategic alliances using the transaction cost economics approach is undertaken in Chapter One of this book.

Agency theory

Agency theory has, as its primary concern, the ability of 'principals' to ensure that 'agents' are fulfilling their objectives. Eisenhardt (1989) pinpoints the contractual agreement between the principal and agent as the central unit of analysis and states that embedded in this theory are a number of assumptions:

i)   that human behaviour is self interested, is subject to bounded rationality and is risk averse

ii) that organizations contain goal conflict among members, that there is asymmetry of information

iii) that information is a purchasable commodity, and principals can secure more detailed information about the conduct of their agents

Accordingly, agency theory focuses on developing the most efficient contract governing the relationship between principal and agent: that is, whether a behaviour-orientated contract is more efficient than an outcome-orientated one. The former includes working to a set of hours, salary, and managerial hierarchy while the latter is based on rewards subject to marketplace (such as stock prices) performance.

The previously outlined Market Power and Transaction Cost Theories largely focus on the position of the organization in its markets (and its ability to manipulate its market to suit its own ends). Neither provide more than a static, one-shot, view of the world and do not develop obligational-contractural relationships and co-evolution in alliances. Agency theory provides a place for self-interest and incentives in analyzing organizations. It draws attention to the implications of contractually framed behaviour under conditions of uncertainty and the need to establish systems to provide the principal with information about the activities of the agent to assist the former to control the latter.

As Child and Faulkner (1998) summarize: 'The principal implication of agency theory is therefore that, just as a principal is advised to put in place a combination of incentives and monitoring mechanisms to ensure that an agent's behavior remains consistent with the principal's objectives, so the partners to a cooperative venture would be advised to make clear to each other the basis on which each will share returns from effective cooperation, and to put into place the systems for information to be shared between them. These provisions should reduce suspicion between the partners and so provide a basis for mutual trust to develop through their working relationship. As and when the partners do trust each other more, so the monitoring mechanisms emphasized by agency theory can become less prominent.'

Increasing returns theory

Increasing returns emphasizes the relationship between factor inputs and returns. Traditional economics presupposes that, past a certain point, increased factor (raw materials, labour and so on) inputs lead to diminishing returns. This view provides for an equilibrium point at which factor inputs are efficiently allocated. But markets do not in fact move to and stay at an equilibrium point but rather the more likely norm is a state of dynamic disequilibrium. That is, markets are always changing and organizations continually need to form new balance points between factor inputs and returns. This tendency is more prevalent in knowledge-based industries where continuing returns are seen. Firms in these (for example, technology) industries can build an early dominance and lock in customers without decreasing returns. Indeed technology-based increasing-returns markets drive firms to form strategic alliances to achieve an early critical mass with which to dominate the market. This view is confirmed by Bettis and Hitt (1995), who assert: 'In industries with a high knowledge content, as opposed to natural resource-based industries, it is uncommon for diminishing returns to occur; instead positive feedback is present where returns continue to increase...the optimum scale may be the entire market and the first mover advantages or an early lead in market share may be quickly magnified into market dominance.'

Game theory

Game theory was originally developed as a mechanism for using the language and analytical power of mathematics to analyze and solve some types of economic events – especially economic decision making or coordination under uncertainty or in the presence of ignorance. According to Rapaport (1961), games vary according to a number of parameters: the number of players (range from two-person versus n-person games), their interests (conflict, coincide, or both), the nature of information access (perfect versus imperfect, complete versus incomplete), the number of times the game is played, the degree of communication allowed between the players and the ability to make promises, commitments or threats.

The most elementary games are two-person, independent decision, unknown outcome games. The type of game attempts to understand the balance between conflicting desires to act selfishly and to act for the common good. Some such games can be extremely poignant, such as the one described by Casti (1992): 'In Puccini's opera Tosca, Tosca's lover has been condemned to death, and the police chief Scarpia offers Tosca a deal. If Tosca will bestow her sexual favours on him, Scarpia will spare her lover's life by instructing the firing squad to load their rifles with blanks. Here both Tosca and Scarpia face the choice of either keeping their part of the bargain or double-crossing the other. Acting on the basis of what is best for them as individuals, both Tosca and Scarpia try a double-cross. Tosca stabs Scarpia as he is about to embrace her, while it turns out that Scarpia has not given the order to the firing squad to use blanks. The dilemma is that this outcome, undesirable for both parties, could have been avoided if they had trusted each other and acted not as selfish individuals, but rather in their mutual interest.'

In this scenario there are two decision making parties, Tosca (A) and Scarpia (B) and both have the choice of cooperating or defecting. The maximum attainable value for each is three and the minimum value is one. Drawing on Child and Faulkner (1998), the possible outcomes of this two person, zero-sum game, from Tosca's perspective, are detailed in Table 3.1 and Table 3.2.

The best option for each individual is option 1 for Tosca and option 4 for Scarpia. For Tosca to cooperate without knowing Scarpia's likely

Table 3.1   Outcomes of Tosca-Scarpia Game

	Tosca (A)	Scarpia (B)	A score	B score	Total
Option 1	defects	Cooperates	3	0	3
Option 2	cooperates	Cooperates	2	2	4
Option 3	defects	Defects	1	1	2
Option 4	cooperates	Defects	0	3	3

Source: Drawn from Child and Faulkner (1998), Analysis

Table 3.2   Actions of Tosca-Scarpia Game

	Tosca	Scarpia	Rifles	Lover
Option 1	Stabs Scarpia	loads blanks	blanks	escapes
Option 2	Submits	loads blanks	blanks	escapes
Option 3	Stabs Scarpia	does not load blanks	not blanks	Dies
Option 4	Submits	does not load blanks	not blanks	Dies

Source: Drawn from Child and Faulkner (1998), Analysis

response is to risk the 'sucker's pay-off' (option 4, score 0, Tosca submits, lover dies), so rationally Tosca should defect and gain either the option 1 (Tosca score 3, lover lives, no surrender) or lesser option 3 outcome (Tosca score 1, stab Scarpia, lover dies). Neither Tosca nor Scarpia have any prior knowledge or insight into how the other will act. If they did, they could cooperate (option 2), both score 2 (lover lives) and raise their total return to 4. The tendency of both Tosca and Scarpia, however, will be to not trust each other and to defect, especially if the 'game' is played only once.

Axelrod (1984) carried out a series of experiments to test the cooperation dimension of game theory over a series of consecutive games. He confirmed that the best strategy was to follow two rules known as tit-for-tat – that is, to cooperate at the start and thereafter to act in the same way as the other player did in the previous round. This approach provides a reward for cooperation, through increased payoffs, and a penalty for defection. As the game is played over time, increased payoffs to cooperation accumulate to both players with occasional corrective penalties for defection.

In a single-play, zero-sum game, the strategy of defection (competition) is the rational one. In a multiple-play, non-zero-sum game, series cooperation is more likely to pay higher yields and is the optimal strategy for both players. To defect, in the latter type of game, means risking one's reputation and the possibility of missing new cooperation opportunities.

The tit-for-tat strategy has inherent disadvantages when applied to reality. No communication in unlikely in multi-play situations such as a strategic alliance. Here what is more likely is that the players (partners in the strategic alliance) will be able to communicate with each other. This, according to Ridley (1996), 'leads them to cooperate with cooperators, return to cooperating after mutual defection, and punish a sucker by further defection, but it assumes that they continue to cooperate after being a sucker in the previous round'.

Game theory has value in assisting attempts to determine choice between competition (defection) and cooperation through a strategic alliance. The theory does, however, presume that the actor in each firm is a single decision maker, not a number of managers with differing perceptions of the alliance or the interface, and assumes that decisions are arrived at through a process of rational analysis and clear information on actions and counter-actions.

Strategic management perspective

This perspective draws attention to the requirement for actual or prospective partners to an alliance to determine a fit between their respective strategies. Such an inter-organizational fit may be at the macro-level, between strategies and national industry environments, or at the micro level, between the organization's internal capabilities, systems, ethos. The former generally commences with an analysis of the rationale for entering into alliances and the choice of partner, while the latter borders on organization theory work.

Harrigan (1988b) asserts that the choice of partner is essentially a rational and analytical process. Contractor and Lorange (1988) in attempting to show this rational process identify seven, variously overlapping, objectives for entering into cooperative arrangements. They are:

i)   risk reduction
ii) achievement of economies of scale and/or rationalization
iii) technology exchanges
iv) co-opting of blocking competition

v)   overcoming government-mandated trade or investment barriers
vi)   facilitating initial expansion of inexperienced firms
vii) vertical quasi-integration advantages of linking the complementary
      contributions of partners in a 'value chain'

Following on Geringer (1991) distinguishes between two types of partner
selection criteria: task and partner related. 'Task-related' criteria have to
do with items such as the internal value chain activities – resources
(finance, competencies, factories, marketing and distribution, institutional environment) while 'partner related' criteria have to do with association competence (culture – corporate or national, past favourable
alliance activities, trust between management teams, structure and size).
Lawrence and ul-Haq (1997) examine the nature of bounded rationality
in the short-listing of a selection of potential alliance partners, a process
that encompasses both task and partner-related factors with the latter
often being prior and primary.

    To sum up the foregoing, market power and transaction cost theories
provide a basis for cooperation as mechanisms for, respectively, increasing monopolistic tendencies and generating extraordinary returns, and
reducing the cost of transactions, thereby allowing reduced prices or
increased margins. Game theory provides a further rational explanation
of the cooperation/competition choice. Strategic management theory
provides for a number of differing reasons for firms to enter into
alliances and allows for the selection and matching of partners taking
into account their external contexts and the match or complementarities
of internal contexts.

Organization perspective

This area of theorizing about strategic alliances is made up of five main
sub-perspectives: population ecology, resource dependency, organization,
organizational learning and trust.

Population ecology theory

Population ecology theory proposes studying populations of firms,
'homogeneous group of organizations in a certain industry' (Aldrich,
1979), and posits that the survival and development of these populations is contingent on their successful adaptation to changes in the
external context in which the organization operates. Such changes lead
to a process of selection of future members dependent on the ability of
current members to adapt to these structural changes in the industry.
Firms that can adapt do so and may survive a natural selection process

and prosper, while firms that cannot or will not adapt are subject to structural inertia. Strategic alliances or cooperative arrangements are responses to uncertainty in the external environment (Aldrich, 1979) and attempts to adapt by reconfiguring available resources and access new resources to meet new needs.

Resource-dependency theory

Resource dependency theory has, at its core, the view that a firm's resources, rather than the products it produces, are defining factors in its competitive position. (Wernerfelt, 1984; Barney, 1991). Resources may be tangible such as manufacturing equipment, factories, computers, offices, staff, or intangible such as intellectual property rights (patents, copyrights, brands, goodwill), knowledge resources (carried in the minds of staff, for example) or other such capabilities embedded in internal processes of the firm.

It follows that this view puts the acquisition, control and utilization of resources in an appropriate manner as primary activities of the firm's management. Resources can be acquired by acquisition or merger along, and through the lengthening of, the value-chain via backward/forward integration or expanding the width of the value-chain through a horizontal merger. Resources can also be grown internally, though this would take longer than the mergers and acquisition (M&A) route. Both the M&A and organic routes provide a high degree of control over resources. In the post-M&A firm the board of directors has direct control over the firm's resources but may well have to deal with a number of issues relating to integration of resources, people, culture and processes. Similarly in organic growth situations the resources are being developed in a mono-culture and set of existing processes and procedures and may be blind to new ideas or perspectives.

With increasing turbulence in the external environment, the organization is continually required, by competitive pressures, to provide innovative products or services to meet ever-changing needs among individual and corporate consumers. This ratcheting-up of the general speed at which innovation needs to take place tends to make M&A and organic growth comparatively slow mechanisms for acquiring resources. Pfeffer and Salanick (1978) assert that scarcity of appropriate resources leads to organizations attempting to exert a degree of influence over firms that have the required resources through engaging in inter-organizational relationships. Partners anticipate that benefits of acquiring these resources will exceed the costs according to Simard (1996).

The resource-dependency view of strategic alliances emphasizes the importance, in effective competition, of the ability to possess a set of core competences (Hamel and Prahalad, 1994) and leads to the view that even when organizations recognize deficiencies in their critical competencies they lack the ability either to develop these competencies or the ability to develop them sufficiently quickly. Entering into an alliance, in order to access the required competencies leads to a fluctuating balance of power between participants that is dependent on control structures, degree and nature of investment and degree of need to access the other partner's resources.

Organization structure and management theory

This approach provides a locus for considering practical issues of how to structure, manage and organize strategic alliances. However, the variety of forms of alliances makes them difficult to analyze, according to Borys and Jemison (1993).

Child and Faulkner (1998) classify the extant literature into three areas;

i)   the relative importance of structure and process in the management of alliances
ii) their network or quasi-network nature
iii) issues of the degree and type control, autonomy and learning

i)   Structure and Process
Doz and Prahalad (1993) argue, in relation to decentralized multinational corporations, that 'one needs a theory that transcends the structural dimensions and focuses on underlying processes...more than the formal structure, the informal flow of information matters. So do the processes of influence and power, such as how the trade-offs among multiple stakeholders and multiple perspectives are made'. As mechanisms for accessing resources in turbulent and fast changing environments strategic alliances are subject to re-configuration more often than multinationals. While formal structures do exist, informal exchange of information needs to be taken into account. Effective bilateral-multilateral information flow is a requisite for developing operational efficiency and effectiveness, cultural (corporate and national) understanding and cohesion and dynamic learning.

ii) Network Nature
Networks are classified by Faulkner (1995) as being 'characterized by a high sense of mutual interest, active participation by all partners,

and open communications'. These networks of firms act as a conduit for sharing knowledge. Indeed while transaction cost theory surmises that alliances act as a mechanism for reducing costs of open market transactions while mitigating rigidities of firms, networks generally exist for resource complementary issues – that is, a network member provides a function which is synergistic with a different contribution from another member of the network (Johanson and Matsson, 1991). These networks provide access to increased production capacity, speed of response to market changes, competencies and resources not owned by a firm, industrial intelligence and information from outside its borders.

As Child and Faulkner (1998) summarize, 'The degree of prominence networks have received has significantly increased in recent years. This is due largely to the globalisation of markets and technologies, leading to the widespread growth of cooperative activity as a necessary strategy, if firms with a limited financial strength, focussed competencies, and limited "global reach" are to be able to compete in global markets. An attractive characteristic of many networks, then, is that they help members to achieve increased global reach at low cost and with a minimum time delay ... They enable synergies between members to be captured, and provide the conditions for the achievement of scale-and-scope economies through specialization.'

iii) Control and Autonomy

Child and Faulkner (1998) address the issue of control in strategic alliances by proposing that 'the collaboration between partners is balanced against the potentially competitive aspects of their relationship, and each partner seeks to reconcile the alliance's activities with its own strategy and pattern of operations. Insufficient control over an alliance can limit a partner's ability to protect as well as efficiently utilize the resources it provides to the alliance, and to achieve the goals it has set for the alliance.'

Organizational learning theory

Organization learning rests on the generally accepted assumption that adaptation to external environmental change and the enhancement of internal capabilities are essential elements of a successful strategy. Both require some form of 'learning' by the organization, that is the embedding of learning in the procedures, precepts and processes of the firm.

Some theories emphasize individual learning, others learning 'by' the organization. In most cases theorists see these as interrelated. De Geus (1988) argues that the primary competitive advantage in the future will be the ability of individual managers of one firm to learn faster than individual managers of a competing firm. Villinger (1996) also stresses learning takes place at an individual level and consists of 'the process of developing a potential to improve actions (behaviours) through better knowledge and understanding (cognition)'. By contrast, Argyris and Schon (1978) find that 'organizational learning is not merely individual learning, yet organizations learn through the experience and actions of individuals'. Like Villinger, Nonaka and Takeuchi (1995) state 'knowledge is created only by individuals and an organization can only support creative individuals or provide suitable contexts for them to create knowledge'. They go on to differentiate between individual and organizational knowledge creation: 'Organization knowledge creation...should be understood as a process that 'organizationally' amplifies the knowledge created by individuals and crystallizes it as part of the knowledge network of the organization. This process takes place within the expanding 'community of interaction' which crosses intra- and inter-organizational boundaries'. Moreover organizations may adopt cooperative strategies as mechanisms to acquire new knowledge. Inkpen (1995) asserts that learning processes between partners are requisites for successful cooperation.

This analysis leads to two main issues:

i)   how to convert individual learning into organizational learning,
ii) how to engender (or withhold) the transfer of learning across intra-firm borders.

i)   Individual versus Organizational Learning

Polanyi (1966) differentiates tacit and explicit knowledge. Tacit knowledge is person specific, often intuitive and embedded in its context. It is difficult to verbalize, to formalize, to communicate to others. Explicit knowledge is codified and can be transmitted across the organization in formal and systematic ways. The conversion of tacit, individual and private knowledge into collective, organizational and shareable knowledge requires codification. Argyris and Schon (1978) assert that organizational learning takes place at a number of levels: 'single-loop', 'double-loop' and 'deutero-learning'. Child and Faulkner (1998) classify these as 'routine improvements', 'reframing of organizational systems and perspectives' and 'learning how to learn'. Table 3.3 illustrates these classification systems.

ii)   Transfer versus Non-Transfer
Barriers to conversion from tacit to organizational knowledge include a lack of awareness of one's tacit knowledge. Some individuals retain control over their knowledge by maintaining it in tacit form and share it with others only through personal interaction and in exchange for other knowledge (in project focussed teams, for example).

The internal structures, strong hierarchical reporting lines and 'Chinese Walls' concept may also dampen transmission of tacit and explicit knowledge across intra-firm boundaries. 'Chinese Walls' are used to describe, for example, explicit, though in practice often permeable, barriers to sharing price-sensitive information between trading and corporate finance departments of an investment bank.

The issue of transfer or non-transfer of tacit or explicit knowledge across inter-firm boundaries becomes a core issue in strategic alliances.

Table 3.3   Levels of Organizational Learning

Levels	Theoretical Approach	Pragmatic Approach
Higher	*learning – 'deutero learning'* learning how to learn so as to improve the quality of the organizational learning process itself	*Strategic learning* changes in managerial mindsets, especially in understanding the criteria and conditions for organizational success
Middle	*reframing – 'double loop'* changes of existing organizational frameworks – involves questioning existing systems – orientated towards survival in changing environmental conditions	*systemic learning* changes in organizational systems, with an emphasis on learning how to achieve better integration of organizational activities
Lower	*routine – 'single loop'* improvements and adjustments to optimize performance within the limits of existing organizational frameworks and systems	*technical learning* the acquisition of new specific techniques such as more advanced production scheduling, or managerial techniques such as more advanced selection tests

Source: Child and Faulkner (1998). Includes Argyris and Schon (1978)

Child and Faulkner (1998) elevate the 'ability to learn' (higher level 'deutero learning' as detailed in Table 3.3) as 'probably the most important intangible asset that a company can possess. Its enhancement is frequently the main motive for entering into collaboration with other companies. Alliances create learning opportunities ...'.

Geringer (1991) notes that a perception of complementarities by alliance partners is a requirement for cooperation to extract benefits of learning from each other so as to compete better with other firms. Partners to an alliance can learn from each other in an attitude of collaboration or competition. In the former, learning may be *from* each other or *with* each other (Inkpen, 1995). In the latter, one partner would not be interested in collaborative learning but rather intends to learn rapidly from the other partner – to cooperate to 'access knowledge which they may subsequently turn to competitive advantage against their partners' (Child and Faulkner, 1998). This dichotomy provides a danger – today's collaborator may be tomorrow's competitor – and thus the decision to collaborate and to transfer knowledge (equally or differentially) can be construed as a Game Theory type decision.

Asymmetric learning in cross-border strategic alliances was stated by Hamel (1991) as being the practical manifestation of this danger – 'managers often voiced a concern that, when collaborating with a potential competitor, failure to "outlearn" one's partner could render a firm first dependent and then redundant within a partnership, and competitively vulnerable outside it. The two premises from which this concern issues seemed to be that (1) few alliances were perfectly and perpetually collusive, and (2) the fact that a firm chose to collaborate with a present or potential competitor could not be taken as evidence that the firm no longer harboured a competitive intent *vis-a-vis* its partner'.

Pucik (1991) observes that 'Organizational learning is not a random process, but a carefully planned and executed set of policies and practices designed to enlarge the knowledge base of the organization. Preventing an asymmetry (or creating an asymmetry in one's favour) in organizational learning is a strategic requirement for firms engaged in competitive collaboration, when technology is transferred between competitors. Win/win outcomes so fashionable in academic literature are not likely to occur with one of the partners placed at a bargaining disadvantage. Not providing a coherent strategy for the control of invisible assets in a partnership is a sure formula for failure.'

Accordingly effective learning between two or more firms in an alliance requires:

i)   intention to learn,
ii) necessary capacity to learn,
iii) ability to convert acquired knowledge into useful resource,

and this is predicated on:

i)   reduction of emotional and cognitive barriers,
ii) reduction in organizational barriers,
iii) openness of inter-organizational communication,
iv) effective circulation of knowledge.

Trust perspective

In the trust perspective, mutual – and often differential or asymmetrical – dependence on a partner or partners is an essential part of an alliance. Trust, 'the willingness of one party to relate to another in the belief that the other's actions will be beneficial rather than detrimental to the first party, even though this cannot be guaranteed' (Child and Faulkner, 1998) is necessary to a successful strategic alliance. As partners invest specific tangible assets into an alliance or allow and encourage transfer of intangible assets (such as knowledge and patents) into a strategic alliance, they put themselves at risk; for example, one might exit from the alliance and use the acquired knowledge to compete with former partners.

According to Creed and Miles (1996), increased trust between strategic alliance partners is beneficial, because trust:

i)   reduces bounded rationality (sharing of information leading to better informed actions and decisions),
ii) provides safer investment in specific assets (trust leading to increased non-transferable investment),
iii) reduces opportunism (trust produces good will, which reduces temptation to take advantage of other partners).

All this results in reduced transaction costs for the partners.

The trust perspective may deal with any of three areas; bases of trust, evolution of trust and social constitution of trust.

Basis for trust

Lane (1998) differentiates between impacts of calculation, understanding and personal identification in such relationships. These broadly equate with stages in the length of time that cooperation has been in place and/or depth of cooperation.

The first stage, calculative trust, 'involves expectations of each other, based on a calculus which weighs the cost and benefits of certain course of actions to either the trustor or the trustee'. This view holds that calculative trust is 'an on-going market-oriented calculation whose value is derived by determining the outcomes resulting from creating and sustaining a relationship relative to the costs of maintaining or severing it' (Lewicki and Bunker, 1996). This is based on the assumption that the cost and penalties for breaking trust are greater than for maintaining it at the formation stage.

The second stage, based on understanding, is the sharing of a common viewpoint or ways of thinking leading to a position where parties to an alliance can predict the other's behaviour towards fulfilment of shared expectations. Lewicki and Bunker (1996) term this type 'knowledge based trust' and note that it 'is grounded in [the] other's predictability – knowing the other sufficiently well so that the other's behaviour is anticipatable'. Here complementary behaviours are based on believing that partners share the same assumptions with regard to the alliance and do not 'defect' in their decisions.

The third stage is based on mutual identification in relation to common purposes. This 'identification based' trust exists because the parties effectively 'understand and appreciate the other's wants; this mutual understanding is developed to the point that each can effectively act for the other' (Lewicki and Bunker, 1996).

Evolution of trust

This provides for the evolution of trust – from calculative, through knowledge-based to identification-based – as a process that is at the core of a strategic alliance. Deeper trust develops as partners to an alliance gain more comfort in their ability to predict behaviour of other partners in a given situation; as greater and greater trust develops, the stronger become links between the alliance partners.

Social constitution of trust

Child and Faulkner (1998) argue that trust 'is necessarily realized, and strengthened, by social interaction, cultural affinity between people, and the support of institutional norms and sanctions'. According to Zucker (1986), this trust is developed first on the basis of past experience, second by sharing common characteristics and third through institutional norms and guarantees to completion of transactions as promised.

Summary of perspectives

The key groups of perspectives detailed above (Economic, Strategy and Organization) provide a set of perspectives, embedded in differing disciplines, that assist in analyzing and understanding strategic alliances. To summarize the perspectives:

The economic theory sub-perspectives consider the subject from a market orientated view:

i)   relative power of the firm in comparison with its competitors (market power theory),
ii) boundaries between the firm and other firms (transaction cost economics theory),
iii) relationships between principals and agents (agency theory),
iv) the input-output relationship and dynamic disequilibrium (increasing returns theory),
v)   a model for making decisions in repeat decision scenarios, like strategic alliances (game theory).

The strategy perspective is largely concerned with the fit between the external market context (global, international, national, industry) and the internal firm context (resources, structure, size, culture) and draws on all the other perspectives.

The organizational theory sub-perspective focuses on issues of structure, control and management:

i)   groupings of firms in specific industries (population ecology theory),
ii) rationale for entering into alliances and the link between managerial control and investments (resource dependency theory),
iii) issues of structure, control, management – that is, how to organize the alliance in a practical and strategic context (organization structure and management theory),
iv) adaptation of the firm to changes in the external context and changes in the internal context (organizational learning theory),
v)   mechanisms by which partners in a continued series of 'games' – that is, a series of decisions to cooperate or defect in the context of a strategic alliance – learn to cooperate and deepen the nature of cooperation through trusting that the other partner/s in the alliance will also cooperate (trust theory).

No one sub-perspective is, by itself, comprehensive, and the sub-perspectives show various degrees of overlap. Used together they may provide a reasonable approximation of the complex reality of strategic alliances and allow the scholar to gain insights into their establishment, performance, evolution and dissolution.

Strategic alliances

The foregoing review has detailed primary groupings of theories used to analyze strategic alliances, a form of business organization that falls in and out of favour as external conditions change. As we saw in Chapter Two, use of strategic alliances to serve business needs of banks, paralleled more recently by other industries, has been subject to life-cycles with the current lifecycle ongoing due to the far reaching effects of changes in technology of business organization.

The latest 'interest-lifecycle', as seen in academic literature, began with the Contractor and Lorange (1988) volume of papers on coopera-tive strategies in international business. Twenty-eight papers in that volume summarized the state of academic analysis of strategic alliances at that time. This 'interest-lifecycle' has grown exponentially. Rather than attempt to review all the extant literature this section will point to key areas of research.

In reviewing academic literature it makes sense to select papers on the basis of influence. This can be determined in various ways. In this review the special editions of three reputable journals, as identified for the UK Research Assessment Exercise (Harzing, 2002), have been chosen:

i)   *Strategic Management Journal,*
ii) *Organization Science,*
iii) *The Academy of Management Journal.*

Core readings have also been selected from three academic conference collections on collaboration with the international perspectives (Asia Pacific, North American, Europe) edited by Beamish and Killing (1997) and the collection that started the current 'interest-lifecycle' by Contractor and Lorange (1988). Additional papers have been included based on their judged relevance or importance.

The review is organized by the topics of conception through to dissolution of a strategic alliance, thus:

i)   conceiving cooperation,
ii) forming cooperation,

iii) organizing cooperation,
iv) evolving cooperation,
v) dissolving cooperation.

In each section the literature is placed under relevant subheadings and summarized at the end. At the end of the chapter the whole will be summarized, a summary carried forward to the start of Chapter Five, the analysis of the interview transcripts.

Conceiving cooperation

Current increase in interest in strategic alliances in the academic realm parallels the increasing instability or the degree of dynamic disequili-birum in the context within which firms operate. The first stage in the life of a strategic alliance occurs when potential partner firms consider cooperation as an appropriate response to business needs to, for example, access resources, products and markets.

Changes in the external context are due to 'globalization...driving an increasing number of industries and segments into a reconfiguration phase where cooperative strategies are essential' (Demers, Hafsi, Jørgensen and Molz, 1997). Korbin (1988) asserts that changes in 'technology, marketing and global integration' explain changes in types of ownership. Horton and Richey (1997) link external with internal, finding that firm level incentives to form technology alliances are based on environmental factors. All the above observations support the view that cooperative strategies allow rapid reconfiguration of the value chain and system at relatively low cost and at reduced risk and that such a strategy also provides lower exit-barriers than a mergers and acquisitions approach.

Context is clearly the key determiner of the decision to use a form of strategic alliance to meet business needs

Stiles (1999), echoing the work of ul-Haq, stresses the link between organization and context, defining networks as 'coalitions between two or more firms, either formal or informal, who share compatible goals, acknowledge a level of mutual interdependence, and are formed for strategic reasons'. Sydow and Windeler (1998) state that interrelations in the broader context are also important: 'network practices are viewed as embedded in the social context of the interfirm network, the industry, and the society, which in turn are produced and reproduced by these practices'. This position is further supported by Bell, Barkema and Verbeke (1997), who add to our understanding of the choice of mode of foreign entry by identifying strategic, transactional, locational and resources-based reasons for the choice. Madhok (1997) expands by asserting that both economizing and strategizing perspectives are essential to a more thorough understanding.

The financial services sector in particular is subject to three trends – deregulation and privatization, new technologies and products and new competitors from overseas and other industries – the impacts of which will 'reduce profits, ...increase market volatility and risk' and lead to an imperative 'to create a super service culture to maintain and grow the business in more intensely competitive markets' (Taylor, 1999). This need will lead to new forms of organization to cut costs, share risks and provide suitable types of products and levels of service.

As the global external context becomes more volatile, so will the industry dynamics, increasing the pressure on firms to reconfigure and to gain access to new resources, products and markets. Alongside this pressure to link this up is the requirement to re-configure rapidly as market and customer preferences change again. The strategic context is thus linked with the industry and firm context. In the particular case of financial services, the drivers are identified as deregulation, privatization, new technologies, new products, new competitors from overseas and from other industries (Taylor, 1999). The strategic alliance allows rapid access and reconfiguration capability.

When determining whether to enter into an alliance, rather than some other form of organization, issues to consider are varied

A primary issue is the required accessibility to assets. Stiles (1997) states that firms enter into competitive mode if resources are mobile or the cooperative mode if resources are immobile or embedded in the firm. This echoes the work of Hennart and Reddy (1997), who note that the method used is dependent on the degree of 'digestibility' of the desired assets; that is, 'joint ventures are preferred over acquisitions when the desired assets are 'indigestible', that is, when they are commingled with non-desired assets'. In their later work Hennart and Reddy (2000) determine that joint ventures (a form of strategic alliance) are preferable to acquisitions when assets are difficult to extricate, post-acquisition management costs would be high, there is difficulty in valuing targets and legal or institutional constraints obtain.

Major strategic reasons for entering into alliances are detailed by Root (1988), who notes that firms enter into alliances when 'incremental net benefits exceed those of open-market transactions or of intrafirm co-operative arrangements that would accomplish the same mission'. By contrast, Contractor and Lorange (1988) determine that firms enter into alliances for reasons of similar or complementary contribution, with mutual dependence being necessary for continuation.

Concerning the process of finding a suitable partner, Osborn and Hagedoorn (1997) encourage a multi perspective approach to the analysis of alliances and networks. This view is supported by Ramanathan, Seth and Thomas (1997), who suggest that the transaction cost perspective needs to be supplemented by other perspectives in any analysis of alliances. In some agreement Lawrence and ul-Haq (1998) find that the effects of 'bounded-rationality' on bankers lead to a pre-listing of potential partners based on a presumed similarity of outlook and organizational culture. Walker (1988) has suggested a guiding framework for this process with strategic, attractive and reciprocity components.

In summary: Strategic alliances are entered into when benefits gained by this method are greater than through another method and in particular where assets that are to be utilized are not easily separable from the firm holding the assets. In finding a suitable partner a number of analysis methods need to be used, not least complementarity of strategy and culture.

A number of factors were identified as pointers towards a successful strategic alliance

Although established firms are more likely to enter into formal cooperation in networks (presumably because of prior positive experience) than less established firms (Ha[o]kansson and Johanson, 1988), technology transfer opportunities can only be gained through rigorous analysis according to Afriyie (1988). Harrigan (1988b) finds that horizontally related partners are more likely to be successful (presumably because of a prior positive relationship) in a strategic alliance than vertically related (buyer-seller) partners.

Barkema, Shenkar, Vermeulen and Bell (1997) note that 'experience with domestic joint ventures and with wholly owned subsidiaries contributed to the longevity of international joint ventures, but prior experience with international joint ventures did not'. Sedaitis (1998) supports this, finding that 'the relational costs of the more concentrated ties increases the cost of search, however it lowers the cost of malfeasance'. These views are echoed by Tyler and Steensma (1998), who considered the impact of prior experiences and perceptions in the assessment of potential technology based alliances and found that executives with positive prior experiences gave more credence to opportunity-based information and lower credence to threat-based information. Baum, Calabrese and Silverman (2000) find support for the hypothesis that start-up biotechnology firms can enhance their initial performance by establishing alliances, forming efficient and diverse networks and allying with established rivals. Reuer and Koza (2000) suggest that 'firms need to contend with both *ex ante* valuation uncertainties and *ex post* integration challenges when assembling resources' for joint ventures.

A number of studies have addressed strategic alliances with regard to foreign countries. In their study of Japanese global companies Anand, Ainuddin and Makino (1997) found that a 'host site [was attractive due to the] availability of labour and investment incentives'. Luo and Chen (1997) noted the need for a good fit between business and investment strategy as a precursor to successful alliances in China. Beamish and Delios (1997a) determined that Japanese firms had a greater propensity to use the joint venture form of strategic alliance than European or US firms. Hérbert and Beamish (1997) drew the conclusion that where 'IJVs are formed to speed up market entry they generally involve fifty-fifty equity splits, and...exhibit relatively high performance rates'. Beamish and Delios (1997b) report that dissatisfaction with performances is 'rooted in a lack of congruity in performance objectives at the time the IJV is formed'. Swan and Ettlie (1997) state that equity joint ventures are more likely to be used in politically sensitive markets if the Japanese partner has knowledge of the product. Saxton (1997) notes that partner firms' benefits are positively correlated with reputation, shared decisions and similarities in strategy. Kogut and Singh (1988) find that strategic choices between greenfield and joint ventures as entry methods into the USA are predicated on the value of the opportunity costs of delays of the former entry method.

In summary: Established firms are more likely to enter into cooperation in networks and horizontally related companies are more likely to be successful than vertically related firms. In Foreign Direct Investment (FDI) situations the equity joint venture was the more likely form and these were more successful if they shared reputation, decisions and strategy.

A number of research findings pointed to the continued use of alliances

Kalmbach Jr. and Roussel (1999) note that 82 per cent of executives, responding to their survey, believe alliances will be the prime vehicle for future growth and that alliances are based on enlightened self-interest and diplomacy. Lin, Yu and Seetoo (1997) determine the main benefits of entering into international joint ventures as the 'motivations of partners, and costs, the contributions they make'.

In summary: Alliances are a force in the mindset of executives and a number of benefits accrue from this.

The next stage is to commence, to action the 'how' and 'where' of the alliance.

Forming cooperation

To commence cooperation requires a number of choices between partners, a risk- reward analysis, a determination of strategic intent and an evaluation of the ability to learn and benefit from and contribute to an alliance.

Researchers point to core processes inherent in a strategic alliance

Dyer (1998a) provides a complicated model of interfirm cooperation: a demonstrated commitment to future action, plus information sharing, plus the use of informed safeguards, equals credibility of one's promise, which in turn leads to reduced transaction costs and increased investment in relation to specific assets, which leads to transaction value through joint performance. This modelling is based on expectations. Doz (1998) draws attention to the expectations of partners and how they 'cover both value creation (the opportunity's potential value and how cooperation between partners will be pursued successfully) and value appropriation (how the partners will equitably share benefits) presumably in proportion to their contributions to the alliance's success'.

Other researchers consider different factors in the formation decision. Ahuja (2000) investigates the propensity of firms to establish interfirm linkages with competitors and finds inducements or incentives to collaborate and opportunities as the two broad classes of factors. Technical and commercial forms of accumulated capital led to attractiveness as an alliance partner. For Anand and Khanna (2000), 'an alliance can be viewed as an incomplete contract between firms, in the sense that detailed interactions between alliance partners can rarely be fully pre-specified'. Doz, Olk and Ring (2000) find that strategic networks may be formed by two paths – the emergent or the engineered (by the triggering entity). Oman (1988) draws attention to the increase in equity joint ventures and contractual interfirm cooperation agreements over traditional foreign direct investment.

In summary: Expectations of alliance partners when entering into an alliance broadly cover how value will be created and distributed.

A number of internal agreements – such as information sharing and demonstrated commitment to action – develop collaboration into performance. Firms possessing technical or commercial capital are attractive partners in what is an incomplete contract where the detail is developed as the alliance progresses.

International alliances add the dimension of cultural dissimilarity

A number of researchers have focussed on the Hong Kong-China dimension. Li and Shenkar (1997) found that the forms of international cooperative ventures in China were dependent on strategic objectives. Pan and Tse (1997) concluded that Hong Kong firms 'are valuable [as cooperation partners] because of their expertise, knowledge and connections in China'. Yeung (1997) provided further insights by drawing attention to the nature of Hong Kong transnational corporations use of at least three dimensions in cooperative strategies: interfirm internalization based on regional ties, interfirm collaboration based on personal friendship, extra firm cooperation based on political patronage.

In summary: In the Chinese context the alliance form is dependent on its strategic objectives and a partner's value is directly related to local knowledge and connections. In Hong Kong, personal, regional and political ties were most important.

Within an alliance a variety of decision-making mechanisms can be used

In considering decision making, Ring (1997) provide a process-outcomes analysis method and Dollinger, Golden and Saxton (1997) find that the processing of reputation in decisions about joint venturing is imperfect. Glaister and Buckley (1997) found that 'the greatest variation in the relative importance of election criteria [task or partner related] occurs with the geographical location of the joint venture'.

In summary: The information on which decisions are made is imperfect and encompasses a number of process-outcome dichotomies.

Organizing cooperation

Once a decision has been made to enter into an alliance, a vast number of issues need to be addressed in order to organize cooperation. Cooperation is an activity which carries with it risks as well as anticipated benefits. Each cooperation requires the opening-up of normally protective boundaries of the firm to the partner or partners.

*The organization and configuration of the alliance attempt to reap the
benefits and mitigate the dangers*

Buckley and Casson (1988) expanded the concept of mutual dependence by defining cooperation as 'coordination effected through
mutual forbearance' – that is, refraining from cheating. Hladik (1988),
concerned about the balance of benefits versus problems in an alliance,
draws attention to the potential positive impact of partner choice and
boundaries and goals on this balance.

When considering operationalizing an alliance, Moxon, Roehl and
Truitt (1988) draw attention to the need for partners to negotiate on
strategic direction and degree of input into such decision making.
Leverick and Cooper (1998) argue that good management practice,
in areas of partner selection, communication, information sharing
and external monitoring, are a substantial part of a successful alliance
relationship.

In an earlier paper, Westney (1988) had called for 'empirical, process
orientated research on how deals [to enter into alliances] are managed
once made'. Supporting this Mayrhofer (1997) expressed concern at
the shortcomings of secondary sources of research. Golden (1997)
states that retrospective data can be inaccurate unless efforts are made
to validate such data, after which it 'provides unique access to past
organizational events'

In summary: Alliances are based on partner firms' mutual
dependence and refraining from cheating, combined with the positive impact of boundaries, partner choice and goals. Appropriate
management practices lead to an increase in performance.

Alliances are complex organizational forms

With regard to the internal organization of a firm, Combs and Ketchen
(1999) propose an integrated view of 'understanding the antecedents
and consequences of organizational actions ... a central theme in
strategic management research'. After surveying 151 firms, Simonin
(1997) concluded that 'experience must be internalised first, and collaborative know-how must be developed for this experience to contribute to future collaborative benefits'. Benefits are considered to be
both tangible (strategic, financial) and intangible (learning or knowledge based). Implementation of an alliance gives rise to content and
process issues, according to Boddy, Macbeth and Wagner (1988).

The relationships between firms are governed by, as Dyer and Singh
(1998) suggest, 'interfirm resources and routines'. These are relation
specific assets, knowledge sharing routines, complementary resources

and capabilities and effective governance which together are sources of competitive advantage. Proprietary knowledge-in-action was the real source of differentiation and hard to replicate by competitors. Olson and Singsuwan (1997) found that performance factors are 'affected by strategic alliance success factors (partnership attributes, communication techniques, and conflict resolution behaviours) to some degree'. In the public goods perspective of Monge, Fulk, Kalman, Flanagin, Parnassa and Rumsey (1998) the two 'goods' are called 'connectivity' (ability of partners to directly communicate with each other through information and communication system) and 'communality' (availability of a commonly accessible pool of information). Connectivity and communality were found in alliances between a number of firms by Jones, Hesterly, Fladmoe-Lindquist and Borgatti (1998). They observed that when members of constellations pursue a collectivist strategy, they focus on their mutual benefits and employ a relational logic. Given these firms' 'need for intensifying relations with partners and clients, constellation members restrict interactions to certain partners and clients and intensify their interactions'. This channelling and distribution of attention of decision makers results, according to Ocasio (1997), in changing behaviours. For Leung, Smith, Wang and Sun (1997), procedural and performance-based distributive justice was related to job satisfaction. Reuer and Koza (2000) argued that, asymmetric information and indigestibility, are complementary in explaining the value of joint ventures, Merchant and Schendal (2000) found that relatedness and R&D orientated activity had a positive impact on the valuation of a joint venture.

The forms of alliances differ as do the purposes. Stabell and Fjeldstad (1998) proposed three generic ways to configure value in firms: chain (transforming inputs of products in interlinking chains), solving (customer problems in refereed shops) and network (linking customers in interconnected networks). Firms in alliances enter into these collaborations so as to realize a 'productive source of value creation and realization' according to Madhok and Tallman (1998). The firm derives resources, social status and recognition from its portfolio of collaborations (Stuart, 2000). The 'competitive aspects of alliances are most severe when a firm's ratio of private to common benefits is high', say Khanna, Gulati and Nohria (1998).

With regard to international alliances Dussauge and Garrette (1999) analyzed alliances by differentiating between features such as multiple decision-making centres, constant bargaining and clash of interests. In establishing international joint ventures in developing countries the participation of the firm and host country institutions is important (Dymsza, 1988) as is the rationale behind it – exploit or invest in know-how, mould or grow operations, fight or produce team effort, externally develop or internally develop joint venture staff.

When considering the value of an alliance, Kaufman, Wood and Theyle (2000) found, as they predicted, that high technology and high collaboration firms, classified as 'problem-solving suppliers', had the largest number of employees and the highest percentage of exports, paid the highest wages and had the highest gross margins of the sample.

In organizing strategic alliances it must be borne in mind that the external environment has a direct impact on the internal environment (Elg, 1998). Elg suggests that the 'original relations of a firm [in a network are] expected to affect its behaviour as the boundaries surrounding its established net of interorganizational relations dissolve' and the impact of external forces increases.

In summary: The internal organization is full of experience capital, a form of intangible capital which links into routines established between one firm and another in an alliance. Connectivity (ability of partners to communicate with each other through information and communication systems) and communality (availability of a commonly accessible pool of information) are at the core of building relationships between partners. Partner firms gain status and recognition from alliances and hope to gain a realized increase in value that can come from transforming inputs, resolving customer issues or linking customers.

Alliance partners deliberately built trust between their firms to facilitate a successful alliance

Inkpen and Currall (1997) found that trust is dependent on prior relationship, risk, forbearance and control. These relational norms, coupled with informal monitoring, are important, according to Aulakh, Kotabe and Sahay (1997), in building trust and achieving performance. As asserted by Holm, Eriksson and Johanson (1997), the commitment to that relationship is positively correlated to its profitability. Again, according to Ari'o (1997) the 'veracity of [a firm] is positively associated with its perception of the partner's cooperative behaviour'.

Sarkar, Cavusgil and Evirgen (1997) provide evidence that 'interfirm exchanges are relationship based, and that competitive advantage lies in the firm's network of associations and exchange ties it shares with its business partners'. These exchange ties require 'procedural justice' or clear, just procedures (Johnson, 1997), to impact on organizational commitment and are based on efficiency in exchange and innovation mediated by relational exchanges, according to Florin (1997). For Sarkar, Cavusgil and Evirgen (1997), competitive advantage 'lies in a firm's network of associations and exchange ties it shares with its business partners'. Alternative governance structures, such as joint ventures, 'impose a greater burden of bargaining and political influence costs than is present in a hierarchy (Pearce, 1997) and short term contracts which, in high technology settings, can lead to long term transfer of learning and firm specific advantages'.

In summary: Trust is considered to be based on prior relationship, risk, forbearance from cheating and control and is built up over time – the greater the commitment to the relationship by both partners in the alliance the greater the profitability. Each firm's perception of and action on the other firm's degree of cooperative behaviour is a core determinate of success.

International collaborations bring increased managerial complexity

After analyzing the cooperation by USA or Japanese large firms with USA technology entrepreneurs, Hull, Slowinski, Wharton and Azumi (1988) conclude that the manufacturing process is the core to advantages being gained. Converting these advantages into reality in, for example, US and European JVs in Japan is fraught with difficulties because of recruitment and staffing, training and development, performance appraisal, compensation and reward system, human resources practice and strategy differences according to Pucik (1988). Research results by Sohn and Paik (1997), in reviewing Japanese firms in Korea, support diversification as an additional control mechanism in international joint ventures. Johnson, Cullen, Sakano and Takenouchi (1997) found that cultural sensitivity is an important factor in strategic integration in Japanese-US alliances. Olk (1997), considering the performance of R&D consortia, concluded that dissimilarity in nationality was positively and research location negatively related to performance. Lyles and Salk (1997) found that 'adaptation mechanisms...were positively associated with the degree to which IJVs reported acquiring knowledge from their foreign parents'.

Different locations led to differing issues in the resulting alliances. Pearce and Branyiczki (1997) focus on the 'clashes in systems of legitimacy' as a mechanism of gaining insights into assumptions brought to Hungarian-Western European collaborations. Papanastassiou and

Pearce (1997) note a high degree of involvement of continental European subsidiaries a parent firms' operations. Tallman, Sutcliff and Antonian (1997) noted that Russian firms use organizational methods to protect their interests in different ways from those of foreign partners.

The internal issues in an alliance depended on the focus of the management of the alliance. Bell, Barkema and Verbeke (1997) add to our understanding of the choice of mode of foreign entry by noting strategic, transactional, locational and resources-based reasons for the choice. Beamish and Delios (1997a) reported that dissatisfaction with performances is 'rooted in a lack of congruity in performance objectives at the time the IJV is formed'. According to Lu and Lake (1997), host country and interparent expectations are usually in conflict and therefore require flexibility in management systems to cope. Dyer (1997) found that 'Japanese automotive transactors minimize transaction costs by minimizing search, contracting, monitoring, and enforcement costs over the long term'. In their research on 112 banks Hopkins and Hopkins (1997) inferred that 'intensity with which banks engage in the strategic planning process has a direct, positive effect on banks' financial performance, and mediates the effects of managerial and organizational factors on banks' performance' and Berg and Hoekman (1988) found that banking, wholesaling and transportation services in the Netherlands benefited from innovation via joint ventures. Pan (1997) discovered substantial differences between Japanese and US equity joint ventures in China, probably due to 'risk orientation, cultural similarities, and impact of political events in China'. In considering the internalization of an international joint venture within one of the parent firms, Reuer and Miller (1997) concluded that valuation depends on the degree of equity held by the parent and debt-cash flow considerations.

With regard to US-Mexican alliances Robins, Tallman and Fladmoe-Lindquist (1998) conclude 'the international parent may achieve the greatest success by providing strategic guidance and key sources of competitive advantage to an alliance, relying upon local partners to take a lead in high cultural content activities such as marketing or labour management'. Makino and Beamish (1999) classified Japanese joint ventures according to location of owners and noted that the strategy should match the ownership structure. Burton (1995b) counterpoises two schools of thought regarding partnering with the Japanese – the Locomotive (Western companies will gain from links with dynamic East Asian companies) and the Juggernaut (wherein

Pacific Rim companies will destroy Western companies and ulti-mately Western economies unless governments step in to arrest their progress). Toral (2000) noted the uniqueness of European-Argentine partnerships. Schaan and Beamish (1988) define a good joint venture general manager in a less developed country as being one who can operate 'constantly within two or more frames of reference and sets of values, and [be] able to successfully manage the idiosyncrasies of their parents'.

In considering valuations in acquire or divest joint venture deci-sions, Chi (2000) noted that whether 'two JV partners can gain from the assets without their partner depends on the extent to which their independently held assets complement those of the venture'.

In summary: Increased managerial complexity in international alliances is due to a number of factors, including differing needs of partners and potentially major differences between internal processes, policies and procedures. In building a cohesive cross-cultural alliance, sensitivity is important, and in R and D Consortia in particular difference of nationality is a positive factor. Differing mechanisms to produce collaboration co-exist, and the choice of method for entering into a foreign market is based on strategic, transactional, locational, resources-based reasons. Poor performance in alliances can be traced to poor performance objective setting at the time of formation. The expectations of the host country and international parent were often different. Over the long term the Japanese build a trust culture to minimize ongoing costs. In the case of banks the strategic planning intensity and innovation via joint ventures have direct positive benefits. There is often a spilt in responsibility between the international parent providing strategic guidance and the local partners taking a lead in high cultural activi-ties such as marketing. A successful joint venture manager operates between two or more frames of references.

Once an alliance has been set in motion, the intents of the partners and the capabilities and organization of the alliance evolve over time in response to both internal and external developments.

Co-evolving cooperation

A strategic alliance is a 'living entity' that is deeply connected with the environment and industry in which it competes. Its development is a function of the co-evolution of member firms, their strategic intents and the ability of the alliance to continue to deliver benefits as compared with a go-it-alone approach.

Kogut (1988) observes that the initial rationale for an alliance changes over time as the alliance develops and that its stability is conditional on the external context – 'it would be foolhardy to view a joint venture as anything but an institutional cooperation of firms within the larger competitive context'. This view is confirmed by Hergert and Morris (1988), who identify the incentive to cheat as the alliance reaches the marketing part of the alliance process, thus 'collaboration becomes more difficult to create and sustain as markets evolve'.

In summary: The external context is in flux. Global, national, regional and product/service markets all change and interact with each other. As this evolution takes place, it becomes increasingly difficult to maintain collaboration.

To maintain the collaboration the alliance partners need to co-evolve.
Learning is at the core of co-evolution in alliances

According to Gomes-Casseres (1988), 'capabilities evolve as firms learn to compete in new industries and become familiar with new environments, and as opportunities for global integration grow', Lyles (1988) underpinned this by considering learning within experienced joint venture firms, and draws attention to the corporate history alliance involvement saying that this adds 'depth to the organization that transcends highly decentralized organization structures'.

In summary: Co-evolution in alliances has at its core the ability to learn and develop new competencies to meet new environmental requirements. Co-evolution will be considered further in Chapter Six.

As alliances evolve, a number of dimensions come into play, with
co-learning often referred to as the most important

The external and internal environment are closely related. Gray and Yan (1997) asserted that stability of a joint venture is dependent on institutional environment, relative bargaining power, any prior relationship and ongoing effects of changes in the political and economic environment. Discussing the internal environment and nature of decision making in international joint ventures Lu and Björkam (1997) found that both competitive strategy and political environment were active roles.

Knowledge transfer is an important issue. While Tiemessen, Lane, Crossan and Inkpen (1997) noted that management of knowledge is predicated on underlying conditions, the intra and inter firm structure and processes and the desired outcomes, Lorange (1997) posited that protection of core competencies of firms in a strategic alliance needed to be well defined as well as 'dynamic to allow the evolution of know-ledge'. Choi and Lee (1997) find that 'incentives and enforcement mechanisms must be established to ensure effective transfer of know-ledge between organizations and to facilitate their continuous strategic change'. Dickson and Weaver (1997) supported a multifaceted view of 'perceived uncertainty', Inkpen (1997) determined that effective knowledge transfer is dependent on a reduction in performance-induced myopia.

New ideas and bargaining power are essential factors. Heracleous (1997) defined the process of strategic thinking as ' to discover novel, imaginative strategies which can re-write the rules of the competitive game: to envision potential futures [synthetic, divergent, creative] significantly different from present'. Inkpen and Beamish (1997) define instability in international joint ventures as a 'major change in partner relationship status that is unplanned and premature from one or more partner's perspectives'. They note that this instability occurs when shifts in relative bargaining power occur and that 'shifts in the balance of bargaining power occur when partners in an IJV acquire sufficient knowledge and skills to eliminate partner dependency and make the IJV bargain obsolete'.

Singh and Mitchell (1996) noted that collaboration assists business survival in one environment yet inhibits adaptation and industry evo-lution. Nti and Kumar (1998) outlined four factors which determine the ability of a firm to learn from an alliance – 'motivational orienta-tion, technological competence, the quality of its human assets and organizational culture'. Inkpen and Dinur (1998) identified 'techno-logy, alliance-partner interaction, personnel transfers and strategic integration' as processes used in transferring knowledge between firm contexts. In contrast, Nti and Kumar (1998) considered differential rates of learning in alliances and found that 'outcome [economic, learning] and process [interaction and psychological satisfaction] discrepancies may emerge as collaboration unfolds' and that these differences occur due to differences in 'absorptive capacity, collabora-tive strategies…and 'how partners assess and react to discrepancies shapes the development path of an alliance'.

The benefits of an alliance vary. Khanna (1998) differentiated between private alliance benefits ('accrue to subsets of participants') and public ('accrue collectively to all participants'). They concluded that collection of benefits and the expectation regarding future benefit streams lead to the intention to learn and develop an 'alliance capability', defined as the 'the firm's ability to identify partners, initiate alliances, and engage in the ongoing management and possible restructuring and termination of alliances'.

Considering success or failure of strategic alliances Larson, Bengtsson, Henriksson and Sparks (1998) found it is crucially dependent on the 'collective learning process'. They develop a typology of learning strategies based on degrees of receptivity and transparency in this process. Koza and Lewin (1998) suggested that research on co-evolution of alliances is missing and proposed that they 'need to be understood and should be researched in the context of the adaptive choices of the firm over time...in this view [alliances] are embedded in the firm's history and strategy portfolio and co-evolve with the firm's strategy, the institutional, organizational, and competitive environment, and the management's strategic intent for the alliance'.

Drawing attention to the pre-eminence of the learning aspects of alliances Inkpen (1998) stated that 'bringing together firms with differing skills, knowledge bases, and organizational cultures, alliances create unique learning opportunities for the partner firms'. Zajac (1998) posited the question of how the relative importance of direct experience, vicarious learning, social forces and firm level alliance competency impact on managers' willingness to undertake alliances rather than merger or acquisition or organic growth routes. Gulati (1998) reported research that 'suggests that social networks of prior ties not only influenced the creation of new ties but also affected their prior design, their evolutionary path, and their ultimate success'. Simonin (1999) highlighted the 'critical role played by knowledge ambiguity' in alliance learning, collaborative ability and duration, while Afuah (2000) found that a 'firm's post-technological change performance decreases with the extent to which the technological change renders co-opetitors' capabilities obsolete'. Kale, Singh and Perlmutter (2000) infer that firms participate in alliances to learn know-how and capabilities from their partner firm while at the same time protecting themselves from the opportunistic behaviour of the partner in acquiring the subject firm's proprietary assets. Inkpen (2000) suggested that firms 'openly acknowledge both asymmetric alliance objectives and an expectation of learning via private benefits'.

In summary: A number of factors (including competitive strategy and the political environment) contribute to stability of a joint venture The structure of the firm determines the management of knowledge and its dynamic evolution. Mechanisms of cooperation (incentives and enforcement) assist continuous strategic change. Strategic thinking allows the envisioning of new rules of the competitive game. Sudden shifts in bargaining power change the dynamics of an alliance and may make it obsolete. Collaboration assists in some environments and inhibits in others, and flexibility is based on the ability to learn. As firms develop the processes of transferring knowledge differential rates of learning occur in outcome and process areas. These discrepancies shape the path of alliances development. The ability to enter into and develop alliances (alliance capability) is predicated on the process on initiating, managing and terminating alliances. The co-learning process, based on receptivity and transparency, is essential to the success of the alliance and is embedded in the history and environment of the firm.

The learning aspects of alliances are crucial. Different firms create different degrees of unique learning opportunities and social networks influenced the creation of ties, development path and success. Technological changes that reduce the appropriateness of the firm's capabilities also reduce its performance. Members of alliances try to learn as much as possible from partners while protecting the transfer of their proprietary knowledge.

Particular firms and countries display particular concerns

Reviewing the knowledge sharing network with Toyota, Dyer and Nobeoka (2000) found that 'learning is facilitated by interorganizational routines that are purposefully designed to facilitate knowledge transfers across organizational boundaries' and mitigate motivation, free rider and cost issues. Naylor and Lewis (1997) concluded that a construction company used the experience gained through an alliance to develop a series of joint ventures within the firm. Human and Provan (1997) found that membership by small and medium sized firms in manufacturing networks can provide 'transactional and transformational' outcomes.

Reviewing alliances in Turkey, Erden (1997) found that widespread use led to high stability. Graham (1988) draws attention to culturally based misunderstandings that arise between American executives operating in Japan, largely due to interpersonal and business relationship differences. When analyzing Sino-Foreign joint ventures, Child, Yan and Lu (1997) found that the degree of foreign influence on management was high, Hoskins, McFadyen and Finn (1997) found differences in learning capability more important than Canadian-Japanese cultural differences.

In summary: Learning is underpinned by specific inter-firm actions, and experience gained can be used to further alliance activity. Networks with smaller firms may lead to new ideas. In overseas alliances cultural differences can lead to misunderstandings in interpersonal and business relations. The impact of foreign influence is high, and learning capability is more important than cultural differences.

Dissolving cooperation

An alliance would only normally exist for the period that it provides appropriate benefits to its members or if it has achieved the objectives set and the business case no longer justifies continuation. At that point the alliance may disband, its intangible or tangible assets internalized by one firm.

Confirming this, Medcof (1997) addressed the question of dissolution in alliances and asserted 'the long-term alliance strategy of the firm focuses primarily on organizational learning of new technical, managerial and partnering skills and on improving organizational positioning in the evolving landscape of alliance activity'. A 25 per cent annual rate of increase in alliance activity in the USA from 1985 to 1992 was noted and the dissolving rate is also high.

Ariño and Torre (1998) reviewed partners in a failed strategic alliance and developed an evolutionary model wherein they 'conclude that positive feedback loops are critical in the evolutionary process, that relationship quality is both an outcome and a mediating variable, and that procedural issues are critical from the start in fostering a climate for positive reinforcement and the building of mutual trust and confidence in the relationship'. Indeed a breakdown of trust was considered a factor in dissolving alliances, as noted by Nooteboom, Berger and Noorderhaven (1997), who state that an 'individual trusts someone when he or she is willing to forego guarantees based on coercion or self-interest', and by Park and Ungson, (1997) who assert that 'opportunistic threat and rivalry appear to be a stronger indication of the dissolution of joint ventures than organizational variables'.

In summary: Alliances survive through organizational learning and repositioning in the environment. Feedback loops and the quality of the relationship are important, and the breakdown of trust is a factor in the dissolution of alliances. Alliances dissolve if they no longer generate a benefit for the partners.

Alliances dissolve as the rationale for their establishment and evolution ceases to exist

Dissolving an alliance may signal the end of its usefulness to its partners, after generating benefits, rather than a failure to generate any benefits. Tyebjee (1988) concluded that the most instability in Japanese joint ventures in the USA occurs when equity ownership is not reflected in board composition; different objectives for growth are seen between the parent firms and the rationale for setting up the joint venture was not clear. Makino and Delios (1997) determined that the 'need for a local partner [in alliances in Asia] declined as parent experience in the host country grows'. Hennart, Kim and Zeng (1998) found that Japanese parent firms displayed a higher tendency to terminate partial ownership (often by selling the shares) of joint ventures in the US as against wholly owned subsidiaries. Si and Bruton (1999) drew attention to the declining performance of international joint ventures in China partly due to unclear knowledge acquisition goals. Echoing this, Barnes, Crook, Koybaeva, Taira and Stafford (1997) determined that social contract differences between Western and Russian business cultures were instrumental in the collapse of Russian alliances. Singh (1997) asserted 'businesses commercializing high and medium-complexity technologies face a higher risk of dissolution than low-complexity businesses'.

In summary: Instability is a function of equity being incongruent with board membership, unclear objectives and rationale at establishment. National differences exist regarding the level of equity preferred. Unclear goals regarding knowledge to be acquired and social contract differences also contributed to dissolution, with high complexity businesses facing a higher risk of dissolution.

Alliances generate different rates of success

Faulkner, Pitkethly and Child (1998) considered post-merger or acquisition change processes in different national contexts and found that US firms absorb the acquisition, that Japanese firms are more concerned with relationships and tacit knowledge transfer, that French firms take strategic decisions at head office and that German firms fail to establish clear post acquisition integration methods. Perhaps this research provides insights into national characteristics and their impact on alliances success.

Dussauge, Garrette and Mitchell (2000) found that partners are more likely to take over link alliances (partners contribute different capabilities) than scale alliances (partners contribute similar capabilities), Merchant (1997) considered the issue of performance, measured by increases in share prices, of international joint ventures and found 'results indicate that participation [of non-manufacturing firms] in IJVs creates economic value on only 40 percent of firms in sample'.

In summary: Different national contexts display different integration methods. Alliances where partner contribution was of different capabilities were more likely to be taken over. Performance of international joint ventures showed a 40 per cent increase in share value in the sample.

Summary

Deregulation, increased use of technology, enhanced and fickle customer expectations, increased merger and acquisition activity, reduction in protectionism, increased formation of trading blocks and global competition all have undermined the old certainties within which firms could aim to achieve a sustainable competitive advantage over a long period. The advent of 'hyper-competition' (D'Aveni, 1994) provides for short run advantage interspersed by frequent interruption with no long run stable end states. Continuous strategic and operational innovation-with-reconfiguration has become the norm. The manager-entrepreneur of Coase (1937) now needs to continuously access and use new tangible and intangible resources to meet the ever-changing needs of consumers and never-ending pressure from innovating competitors. Markets no longer tend towards an equilibrium position but rather are continuously in a state of dynamic disequilibrium. Strategic alliances provide a mechanism for rapid and repeat re-configuration to meet the external and internal changes.

This chapter has provided a review of the development of the strategy field, major perspectives used in analysis of strategic alliances and a summary of key academic papers published on the subject. In detailing economic, strategic management and organization theory perspectives, the review adds to our understanding of the life-cycle of strategic alliances (from conceiving, forming, organizing, evolving to dissolving) in the commercial world. The earlier section on 'Strategic Alliances' has provided a review of key literature on strategic alliances. A concluding summary of this is provided in Table 3.4.

Chapter Four will report on the broader picture regarding the use of alliances by European banks.

Table 3.4   Key Issues in the Literature

Section Title	Sub-Section Title
Conceiving Cooperation	Context is clearly the key determiner of the decision to use a form of strategic alliance to meet business needs
	When determining whether to enter into a strategic alliance, rather than some other form of business organization, issues to consider are varied
	A number of factors were identified as pointers toward a successful strategic alliance
	A number of research findings pointed to the continued use of alliances
Forming Cooperation	Researchers point to core processes inherent in a strategic alliance
	International alliances add the dimension of cultural dissimilarity
	Within an alliance a variety of decision-making mechanisms can be used
Organizing Cooperation	The organization and configuration of the alliance attempts to reap the benefits and mitigate the dangers
	Alliances are complex organizational forms
	Alliance partners deliberately build trust between their firms to facilitate a successful alliance
	International collaborations bring increased managerial complexity
Evolving Cooperation	To maintain the collaboration the alliance partners need to co-evolve
	As alliances evolve a number of dimensions come into play with co-learning often referred to as the most important
	Particular firms and countries display particular concerns
Dissolving Cooperation	Alliances dissolve as the rationale for their establishment and evolution ceases to exist
	Alliances generate different rates of success

4
Broad European Perspectives

Introduction

This chapter reports, summarizes and discusses the outcome of the 44 questions contained in the questionnaire. A comprehensive review of the research methodology is provided in Appendix 1. The observations below are based on the Descriptive Statistics – Frequencies analysis, carried out using SPSS for Windows.

Strategic alliances – a definition

In Chapter One an *ex ante* definition was proposed for a strategic alliance (ul-Haq *et al*, 1996), that is, *A durable relationship established between two or more independent firms, involving the sharing and pooling of resources to create a mechanism (corporate or otherwise) for undertaking a business activity or activities of strategic importance to one or more of the partners for their mutual economic advantage.* It was noted that the alliances defined in this form would constitute the subject of this study.

The definition was provided to the recipients of the postal questionnaire in the covering letter and a set of questions asked to identify the respondent's views as to the validity of the definition.

The respondents were asked:

In respect of strategic alliances you have entered how important do you consider the following possible characteristics to be?

The scale used here and throughout such questions was 'extremely important', 'very important', 'somewhat important', 'not very important' or 'not at all important'.

Durability

Of 59 responses received, a substantial number considered durability to be a 'very' (57.6 per cent), 'extremely' (23.7 per cent) or 'somewhat' (16.9 per cent) important characteristic of a strategic alliance. Only a small number disagreed and responded that durability was 'not at all important'. There is, therefore, substantial support from the respondents for the contention that durability, *ex ante*, is an integral characteristic of a strategic alliance.

However, the issue of duration is a complex one. Embedded, and often made explicit, in the decision to establish a strategic alliance between two firms, for example, is the understanding that their strategic intents are served, at least initially, by entering into the alliance. Both firms expect to gain some advantage through the alliance whether the advantage is offensive or defensive. At time zero the strategic intents of the partners are co-aligned. As the alliance moves from time zero onward, the alliance partners' *strategic intents co-evolve*.

Durability (*ex post*) is not absolute but rather conditional, predicated on the firms entering into a strategic alliance receiving the anticipated gains that the alliance is presumed to be able to generate for them, a collaborative advantage when competing with other firms in their competitive space. Further, they hope this newly formed alliance will repay the effort in establishing it by generating these advantages over a period of time. This will only be realized if the alliance is also sensitive to changes in strategic intent of the member firms and co-evolves to meet these needs.

There is a difference between 'anticipated' and 'realized' durability. It is possible for a strategic alliance to have an anticipated durability (*ex ante*), which may also be for a finite period or limited life-span, on inception but for either or all partners to exit from the strategic alliance at a later stage if a change (*ex post*) in, for example, the conditions of competition or own firm strategic intent occurs.

The very high importance attributed by respondents to the issue of durability probably reflects a wish that the strategic alliance will continue to co-evolve and deliver a collaborative advantage to the member firms, repaying the effort and resources invested in it.

Sharing or pooling of resources

A high number of the 59 responses considered that the sharing or pooling of resources was 'very' (64.4 per cent), 'somewhat' (25.4 per cent) or 'extremely' (6.8 per cent) important. A very small number viewed this as 'not very important'. There is substantial support for the contention that the sharing and pooling of resources is an integral characteristic of a strategic alliance.

Firms that enter into strategic alliances do so because they believe that their strategic intents will be better served together than separately. This often requires some form of sharing and pooling of resources. It may be through the endowment of a new joint venture company with tangible or intangible assets or alternatively through allowing 'claims to usage' by the alliance partners on the member firms' assets and capabilities, including embedded and explicit knowledge.

Creation of a separate company

While the majority of the 59 respondents to this question viewed creation of a separate company 'somewhat' (40.7 per cent), 'very' (15.3 per cent) or 'extremely (3.4 per cent) important', a substantial remainder considered it as 'not very' (30.5 per cent) or 'not at all (10.1 per cent) important'. There is clear support for the contention that a cooperation mechanism needs to be established but that it does not necessarily have to be in the form of a separate company.

This broadly balanced split reflects the variety of inter-organizational structures available to be utilized by strategic alliances. In the BNP/ Dresdner strategic alliance (discussed in Chapter Five), for example, a number of forms were used in co-existence: a global agreement to cooperate, the linking of technology, cross-border marketing and introductions, and the setting up of joint venture companies in Eastern Europe. These various inter-organizational structures were a result of the strategic intentions of the alliance. Each type is considered appropriate to deal with a particular set of objectives. They portray a number of risk versus reward balances and a number of types may co-exist and may change over time.

Indeed the first order decision is that the alliance firms' strategic intents are served by a cooperative relationship and the second order decision is what form – joint venture or non-joint venture – the cooperation should take.

Strategic importance to partners

A substantial majority of the 58 responses to this question held that this characteristic was 'very' (50.0 per cent), 'extremely' (22.4 per cent), or 'somewhat' (15.5 per cent) important'. Only a small number responded that it was 'not very' (10.3 per cent) or 'not at all

(1.8 per cent) important'. There is clear support for the contention that strategic importance to partners is an integral factor in a strategic alliance as one would anticipate.

This reflects the fact that the nature of a strategic alliance entered into is to provide a strategic advantage to the members as compared to non-members.

Mutual economic gain

Of 57 responses to this question a substantial number viewed mutual economic gain as a 'very' (52.6 per cent), 'extremely' (28.1 per cent), or 'somewhat (17.5 per cent) important' characteristic. Only a small number considered this criteria 'not very important'. There is clear support for the contention that mutual economic gain is important in strategic alliances.

Own firm economic gain

Out of 57 responses received for this question, a substantial number of respondents viewed own firm economic gain as 'very' (59.6 per cent), 'extremely' (31.6 per cent), or 'somewhat (7 per cent) important' characteristic. Only a small minority considered it 'not very important'.

The previous two characteristics display the same overall view. That is, a strategic alliance has to generate economic gain for all the members to be of value. This value may not be equally distributed; and it must be noted that respondents, as one would expect, rank their own firm's economic gain higher than that of their partner or partners.

This question and response has embedded in it the nature of the firms under investigation in this book – European banks – that is, common actors which carry out their activities in economic space and see the world in terms of economic gain. If the same question was posited to the National Health Service, the response could well be different, with the strategic intent being to maintain health, alleviate suffering and enhance the quality of life, say, rather than to generate a financial return.

Other

A total of six responses were received. This category encouraged the respondent to suggest additional characteristics of a strategic alliance that they considered important.

These reported characteristics can be broadly placed under four headings: relationships, resources, loyalty and markets.

Relationships

i)   the creation of a strong bond for the (finite) length of the alliance (extremely important)
ii) the long-term commitment to the market and the strategic alliance.

These responses reflect the diversity of the notion of durability in strategic alliances. The first response points to the development of a strong relationship, or bond, between the firms for the duration of the strategic alliance, whatever that period may be. The second takes the opposing view that a strategic alliance is, by its very nature, a long-term commitment to both a partner and a market (one that may be product or service or geographical). This dichotomy will reflect the particular characteristics, and motivations, of the strategic alliances entered into by the respondents.

Resources

i)   the creation of, and access, to increased and specialized resources (very important).

The firms in a strategic alliance may create, through collaboration, a new form of resource that each individual firm may not have in its existing resource portfolio. For example, the sharing of knowledge may lead to innovation and the creation of a new product, service or process. In addition each firm may have specialized capabilities, and cooperation allows an exchange of, or affords access to, these capabilities.

Loyalty

i)   the need for exclusivity among partners (very important),
ii) the need for limited competition on each member's home market (somewhat important).

The former and latter are linked by the concept of mutual commitment. The former may suggest a focussed strategic alliance in which, for example, a retail bank and an insurance company ally, and life assurance products are sold through the bank's retail distribution channels (branch, direct mail, telephone, internet *et al*). Such an agreement would be exclusive (perhaps due to regulatory controls in this product sector, for example) but might allow scope for a further parallel strategic alliance with a general insurance company to expand the offered product range.

An example of the latter might be a cross-European strategic alliance, such as the conception of Scandinavian Banking Partners, where the membership is configured so there is a limited overlap between the geographical areas of competition and the mutual use of partners' networks to deliver cross-border services to their customers.

Markets

i)   the targeting of third countries only (very important),
ii) the provision of an all embracing product range (very important),
iii) market, or regulatory, restrictions.

The first item relates back to Loyalty as above, in that collaboration is restricted to new entry to third countries, with competition continuing in first countries. An example would be two European banks setting up joint ventures in Eastern Europe as a method of entering a new geographical market while continuing to compete in the rest of the world.

The second item refers to the concept of a bank increasing the revenue per customer by encouraging the customer to source all their financial service needs from the main relationship bank. Thus the bank has to be able to offer a full range of services, some of which may be sourced via strategic alliance partners.

The third item connects to the regulatory restrictions imposed on banks entering into new geographical, product or service markets. These may include, in the former case, a requirement that to enter into joint venture in a particular country a minimum level of local ownership is necessary or in the latter case being subject to industry or legal requirements to train salespeople to certain standards. One respondent mentioned the SE Asia region and noted that entry was possible only, in some instances, by means of a joint venture or a strategic alliance with a local partner. In addition, managerial issues included the gaining of access to distribution channels, access and availability of banking licences, minority versus majority shareholding, long-term commitment to the market and the desirability of a local partner.

In addition to the 68 completed questionnaires, a total of ten bank representatives responded that the questionnaire was not applicable to them and therefore did not complete it. The reasons given for non-completion, some of which overlap, are contained in Table 4.1.

Of the ten non-completes half specifically noted that they had no strategic alliances *as defined* in the survey's covering letter and three noted that they had no strategic alliances. In the questionnaire there was space provided for respondents to note their comments, but

Table 4.1   Reasons of Non-Completion of Questionnaire

Reason Given	Number of Banks
Do not have strategic alliances	9
Do not plan strategic alliances	3
Do not have a plan 'durable' relationship	1

all declined to propose an alternative definition or characterization of a strategic alliance.

One French bank's London office noted that they do not expect to enter into durable relationships with other lenders but instead '... expect to join with others, including competitors, from time to time, for particular tranches of business, but would not see it as a continuing relationship except on an *ad hoc* and opportunistic basis'. A German bank official noted that they 'expand ... business activities basically by takeovers or taking majority stakes in partners. Strategic alliances play no significant part in expanding the business activities ...'.

In the view of a number of strategic managers, homogeneity was unlikely rather a varied nature of cooperative activity between commercial organizations and diversity in the form, nature, purpose and importance of such strategic alliances was prevalent.

There are vast differences among firms, depending upon a number of factors. These include the range of options available to generate competitive advantage, the degree of expertise in establishing and managing alliances ('alliance-ability'), the willingness to use cooperative strategies such as strategic alliances and the degree of control that firms wish to exercise over their activities. Nevertheless, the major constituent parts of the definition of a strategic alliance (ul-Haq *et al*, 1996) mooted at the start of this book and embedded in the research have been found to have a high degree of support from the respondents of the questionnaire (classified as over 70 per cent of respondents stating that the characteristic was 'extremely', 'very' or 'somewhat important'). These characteristics are durability, sharing or pooling of resources, creation of a mechanism, strategic importance and mutual economic advantage.

The rationale for conceiving strategic alliances

Strategic alliances are entered into for a wide range of reasons. This section of the questionnaire asked respondents to state how important they considered five reasons for entering into strategic alliances in the banking sector: the reduction in the cost of capital, the sharing of risks, entry into a new product market, entry into a new geographical market and accessing of new distribution channels.

Respondents were asked: 'How important are the following reasons for entering into a strategic alliance?'

'Capital cost reduction'

Of 63 responses, the majority considered capital cost reduction to be 'somewhat (30.2 per cent), 'very' (23.8 per cent) or 'extremely (9.5 per cent) important'. The remainder viewed this motivator as 'not very' (25.4 per cent) or 'not at all (11.1 per cent) important'. On balance the reduction in the cost of capital through entering into strategic alliances was a factor in choosing the alliance route but not an overwhelming one.

There is a general presumption in banking firms that reducing the cost of capital is a desirable goal, as testified to by the majority of respondents. However, the responses were skewed in favour of the 'somewhat important' classification with a high 'not very important' classification.

It should be noted that the pressure on capital in the banking sector is lower than in other industries and is reduced by three factors:

i)   the nature of the subject firms, that is large European banks, with, in the main, easy access to the global bond and equity markets at fine rates,

ii) a sector, banking, that has the highest allocation and utilization of global capital,

iii) a high profit generation among the major banks coupled with a lack of profitable expansion opportunities leading to a surplus of under-utilized retained earnings and resultant share buy-backs (for example, Barclays and Nat West).

On balance, reduction in capital usage is not a major issue for these respondents.

'Sharing risks'

Of 64 responses, a clear majority considered the sharing of risks as a 'very' (37.5 per cent), 'somewhat' (31.3 per cent) or 'extremely' (10.9 per cent) important reason for entering into strategic alliances. Only a majority held the opposing view that this criteria was 'not very' or 'not at all' important. The sharing of risks is therefore a significant characteristic of strategic alliances.

Risks to be shared may be tangible, such as the loss of capital inserted into a new venture; or they may be intangible, such as the loss of reputation if the venture fails. An alliance with an export partner may reduce the likelihood of failure. In European Union countries changes in legislation have enabled European banks to market their products and services in other member countries. The local bank, for example in the UK, has an extensive knowledge base about legislation, distribution systems, consumer preferences and segments, pricing and competition in the UK. When entering into another European country, the UK banks face a new set of risks generated through information asymmetry and mitigate these risks through allying with a local firm. This alliance may act as a low risk – learning, risk identification and market potential gauging – experience prior to a full entry.

'Entering a new product market'

Of 62 responses received on this topic a high number viewed this reason for entering into a strategic alliance as 'very' (46.8 per cent), 'extremely' (19.4 per cent) or somewhat (12.9 per cent) important'. A minority considered it an unimportant reason. Therefore entering a new product market is a significant driving factor for entering into a strategic alliance.

The partners may, for example bring specific product manufacturing, processing and distribution knowledge to the alliance. Many alliances allow the front, customer facing, firm to market a new product which is manufactured and processed by another, non-customer facing, firm, thereby combining the customer relationship with processing knowledge and capability.

'Entering a new geographical market'

Of 64 responses received, the majority consider this reason 'very' (40.6 per cent), 'extremely' (20.3 per cent) or 'somewhat (14.1 per cent) important'. The remainder viewed this reason as 'not very' or 'not at all' important. Entering into a new geographical market is thus a significant reason for entering into a strategic alliance.

The local partner may bring knowledge, access, contacts, and locally based resources and may smooth regulatory hurdles.

'Accessing distribution channels'

Of 63 responses, the majority considered this reason 'very' (46 per cent), 'somewhat' (23.8 per cent) or 'extremely' (19 per cent) important. The small remainder held the view that this reason was 'not very' or 'not at all important'.

On the face of the above aggregate results, accessing distribution channels may be said to be a significant factor in entering into strategic alliances; but is not substantiated due to a typographical error in the questionnaire. In the initial mailing to UK banks, resulting in 17 responses, the question read *'Assessing* Distribution channels'. This error was corrected to read *'Accessing* Distribution Channels' in the subsequent mailing to continental European banks, resulting in 51 responses.

The primary reasons, in the European banks surveyed in research, for entering into strategic alliances are sharing risks and entering into a new product or geographical market.

The rationale for forming strategic alliances

The decision to form a strategic alliance has a number of dimensions. Three questions regarding the formation of alliances were asked in the questionnaire and related to the degree of activity, the propensity to enter into alliances with competitors and the control versus influence issues.

'How many strategic alliances does your company have?'

Of 58 responses, a majority of 67.2 per cent stated they had between one to four alliances. Of the remainder, 22.4 per cent had between five to nine, 5.2 per cent between 10 to 15 and 5.2 per cent enjoyed more than 15. The question elicited a general response that displays a tendency towards a smaller number of strategic alliances.

The question does not differentiate between 'serial-alliancers' who maintain a limited number of relatively short-term alliances and 'parallel-alliancers' or 'compulsive-alliancers' who, as a matter of preference, effectively outsource production, operations or distribution through the strategic alliance route. It also does not differentiate between large global alliances or smaller intra-country alliances.

'We do or are willing to enter into strategic alliances with our competitors'

Of 60 responses, the majority either 'agree' (51.7 per cent) or 'strongly agree' (6.7 per cent) with this statement. A figure of 23.3 per cent 'neither agree or disagree' and the remainder 'strongly disagree' (10 per cent) or 'disagree' (8.3 per cent). The majority are willing to enter into strategic alliances with their competitors.

In the sector (banking) and segment (large European) under analysis, the majority of participants will be competitors in one area or another – product, service, customer segment, geographical location and so on. The impetus on collaboration is to find areas of mutual benefit while continuing to compete in other areas – a hybrid or Composite Strategy (Burton, 1995a).

'We consider that there is a direct positive relationship between ownership, in equity terms, and management control and influence in strategic alliances'

A total of 68 responses were received. Of these a majority 'agree' (55.9 per cent) or 'strongly agree' (20.6 per cent) with this statement. A small number (17.6 per cent) of respondents 'neither agree nor disagree' and an even smaller number (5.9 per cent) 'disagree'. There is a clear view that this relationship between ownership and control holds.

Indeed it is a factor of the nature of publicly quoted companies that the degree of equity ownership determines the number of votes under one's control or influence which is available, but not necessarily used, at a firm's Annual General Meeting. In many alliances, however, no equity relationship exists and the control and the degree of influence over resources and direction is negotiated between parties to the alliance. This negotiation is either through contractual agreements or on a continuous basis and depends on the degree of congruence between the strategic intents of member firms and the alliance.

The rationale for organizing strategic alliances

An alliance has to be actively managed to be effective. The locus and nature of strategic alliance management may differ from that of the internal hierarchies of the partner firms and will need to address the probably differences in the work and priority cultures of these member firms.

A number of questions regarding the management of alliances were asked in the questionnaire

'We consider our strategic alliances have met or are meeting our strategic objectives'

Of 65 responses received, a majority either 'agree' (61.7 per cent) or 'strongly agree' (18.3 per cent) with this statement. A minority 'neither agree nor disagree' and 'disagree' and 1.7 per cent 'strongly disagree'. The majority of respondents clearly thought that their strategic alliances have or are meeting their strategic objectives.

These responses may reflect a lifecycle view of the alliances. Successful alliances may be at the start of the lifecycle, with initial objectives being met, or may be well established, with the ongoing and final objectives being met. Alliances regarding which 16.7 per cent of respondents stated 'neither agree nor disagree' to the above question may be in the start and middle phases of the lifecycle (that is, it is too early to make a judgement) while the 'failed' alliances (those which have not been successful (or have been fully successful) in meeting the strategic objectives of the partners) may well have been disbanded.

The skew is for successful strategic alliances and may be reflective of the wider experience of alliance partners of successful outcomes or may be due to the skew in respondents. That is, those banks that chose to respond to the questionnaire, by completing and returning it, were those that had a generally positive experience of alliances. Those with a generally negative experience may have declined to return the questionnaire.

'The objectives of our alliances are specific'

Of 61 responses received, a large majority made up of 'agree' (52.5 per cent) or 'strongly agree' (44.3 per cent) with this statement.

Indeed the decision to enter into a strategic alliance is generally a positive decision to gain access (or deny other competitors access) to resources, markets, knowledge and so on through alliances. Prior to this decision the firm must have pre-identified (broadly or narrowly) this need. The strategic alliance is usually a conscious choice, an outcome of this process, and thus reflects these pre-existing, and generally specific, objectives.

'Our strategic alliances identify and undertake specific tasks in support of these objectives'

Of 61 responses agree (60.7 per cent) or 'strongly agree' (36.1 per cent) with this statement. A tiny number 'neither agree nor disagree'. A clear majority of respondents overwhelmingly agree that their strategic alliances identify and undertake specific tasks in support of these objectives.

The level of response reflects the responses in the previous question and is an outgrowth of the 'management by objectives' view embedded in the respondent's strategic alliances.

'We encourage our strategic alliances to take calculated initiatives'

Of 61 responses a majority made up of 'agree' (49.2 per cent) or 'strongly agree' (16.4 per cent) while the remainder 'neither agree nor disagree' (27.9 per cent) or 'disagree' with this statement.

A much lower percentage broadly agreed with the view that strategic alliances are encouraged to take calculated initiatives than those (in the two previous questions) who agreed with the statements about specific objectives and specific tasks.

This finding may imply that firms managing alliances simultaneously ask for specific objectives and tasks while allowing a varied degree of calculated initiative in pursuit of these.

This may be reflective of the nature of the relationship between the firm's internal dynamics and its decision to enter into a strategic alliance. A firm may host a range of concurrent behaviours – management by objectives, engendering continuous innovation, taking calculated risks, underlying or occasional lethargy, developing emergent strategies, imposing strategic intents, suffering external discontinuous shocks. The strategic alliance, on the other hand, is generally set up to fulfil a specific need of the partner firms – perhaps to fill a resource or access deficiency. During the lifetime of the alliance it may be subject to many of the behaviours of the partner firm(s) but the balance may be different. Managers of the alliance will also be empowered to act with a varied degree of independence, from the member firms, in achieving the overall outcomes desired by the member firms.

'We are strongly committed to our strategic alliance partners'

A total of 61 responses were received. Of these the majority 'agree' (47.5 per cent) or 'strongly agree' (18 per cent) with this statement. The remainder 'neither agree nor disagree' or 'disagree' with this statement.

While the majority agree with this statement, we saw, however, earlier in this chapter that mutual economic gain and own firm economic gain are 'very', 'extremely' or 'somewhat important' factors in a strategic alliance. If the strategic alliance meets these overarching economic gain objectives, then the commitment obtains. If not, the degree of commitment would probably be reduced. This latter view of conditional commitment is reflected in the smaller who 'neither agree nor disagree' with the statement and further supported by the smaller number of respondents who 'disagree'. The last group are even more likely to change alliances if the external economic rationale changes.

'When entering into a strategic alliance we devote substantial time to establishing methods for making decisions'

Of 61 responses a high majority of 'agree' (65.6 per cent) or 'strongly agree' (18 per cent) with this statement. The remainder 'neither agree nor disagree' or 'disagree' with this statement.

Strategic alliances may, for example, have a concrete tangible form through a joint venture or a more diffuse form through a cooperating mechanism. The joint venture will have its own board of directors and the balance of power would generally reflect the shareholding in the joint venture by the strategic alliance partners. A non joint venture cooperating mechanism would require a contractual agreement or *ad hoc* arrangements. Contractual agreements may delineate the level of claim to mutual resources, profit sharing, decision-making processes and so on all of which will have to be discussed, negotiated and codified. *Ad hoc* arrangements will require an agreement about the process of decision-making and intensive negotiation prior to a decision being made. All require an investment in the processes of making decisions.

Agreement on the decision making process is particularly relevant and important where there are significant differences in culture between the partners. Such differences may be due to size (large international and small regional), product expertise (retail bank and an insurance company), ethos (investment bank and commercial bank), regulatory structures (life assurance and funds management), linguistic expertise and embedded presumptions (French and German), national culture and ethos (Brazil and the UK).

The rationale for co-evolution in strategic alliances

The concept of co-evolution can describe the evolution of 'national contexts' and the 'zones of manoeuvre' available in these national contexts, Clark (2000). At the next level down, this concept may be used to analyze geographically determined regional or industry contexts and further, at the increasingly micro level, the individual firm. In this chapter co-evolution is used in this latter firm level context.

At the start of an alliance the strategic intents of the member firms can be said to be co-aligned – that is, facing in a similar direction with a similar intent. As an alliance moves through time, the external environment, internal drivers for all partner firms, and the drivers for individuals and the projected outcomes involved in the alliance (especially if in the form of an independent joint venture) co-evolve and may converge or diverge in varied combinations as discussed in Chapter Five.

Questions about this evolution process were asked in the questionnaire.

'When entering into strategic alliances we devote substantial time to establishing methods for monitoring the implementation of decisions'

Of 61 responses a majority 'agree' (52.5 per cent) or 'strongly agree' (18 per cent) with this statement. The remainder 'neither agree nor disagree' or 'disagree' with this statement.

It follows from the above discussion about managing, that in the complex environment of a strategic alliance it is important for partners to monitor the implementation of decisions. This is especially important because implementation may take place within one firm, a joint venture for example, while the broad decision was made by more than one firm. There may not be direct control of the activities of the alliance by member firms, rather a monitoring and influencing of activity may be the appropriate form of management.

'When entering into strategic alliances we devote substantial time to establishing a method for resolving conflicts'

Of 61 responses the majority 'agree' (55.7 per cent) or 'strongly agree' (14.8 per cent). The remainder 'neither agree nor disagree' or 'disagree' with this statement.

A significant majority agreed with this statement. Conflicts that arise in a joint venture can be resolved in a board meeting. In a more diffuse non joint venture however, a mechanism for resolving conflicts needs to be established. This may be through a coordinating committee, for example. Such a mechanism is essential to the process of allowing the strategic alliance to co-evolve with the strategic intents of member firms.

'When entering into strategic alliances we devote substantial time to establishing ... a number of other issues'

Out of 61 responses, a small number, eight, made additional comments under this section. These observations related to three headings: commercial benefits, marketing and dissolution.

Commercial benefits

Some respondents referred to the optimizing of commercial action, sharing profits/benefits, and the legal and tax framework. As strategic alliances have at their centre the need to obtain a competitive advantage (or mitigate a competitive disadvantage), all three factors above are clearly important. The third factor is particularly important in the case of cross-border alliances or third country operations.

Marketing

Some respondents referred to methods for promoting the alliance to customers and to methods for enhancing the relationship with the partner. The former is important in engendering cross-selling of products and services to each other's customer base, and the latter is both an immediate and ongoing need.

Dissolution

A respondent referred to methods for breaking the alliance. Strategic alliances, as was seen earlier in the managing section, are set up to meet specific objectives. When the alliance no longer meets those objectives or cannot evolve to meet new, revised objectives, it may need to be dissolved. An orderly dissolution and withdrawal is preferable to its opposite and may need to be carried out according to predetermined and perhaps pre-documented procedures. The procedures may delineate details such as providing the first refusal of the partner's shareholding to the other partner(s), the split and distribution of resources and profits, and non-competition agreements.

The dissolution of a strategic alliance may well be a positive step. Take the example of a UK firm entering a new geographical market via a strategic alliance with a local partner in Spain. Over time the UK firm would gain knowledge about local business conditions and would also build up its contacts and relationships with distributors (wholesale and retail), while the Spanish firm gains access to knowledge of new products and services. The UK firm may decide to go it alone in the Spanish market by buying out its local partner. The strategic alliance, though dissolved, would have to have met the UK firm's objective of entering the Spanish market and may also have met the Spanish firm's objective of gaining a knowledge transfer.

Current status of strategic alliances

This section of the questionnaire asked respondents to provide information about the current geographical distribution of strategic alliance partners.

A total response of 68 completed questionnaires was possible. The responses are tabulated and discussed below. The 'percentage' is the number of responses received as a percentage of the total number of responses to that particular question (for example, 18 equals 100 per cent).

'How many of your strategic alliances are with partners in the following regions – UK?'

Table 4.2 provides details of the responses. The preference is to have one strategic alliance with a partner in the UK. This may reflect the highly concentrated nature of the UK banking sector in the hands of HSBC, NatWest, Barclays and Lloyds TSB. Where there is more than one UK alliance, this may relate to UK-to-UK alliances. The rationale for these alliances may be due to the trend, initiated in the 1980s,

Table 4.2   Number of Partners in UK

Number	Frequency	Percentage
1	6	33.3
2	2	11.1
3	2	11.1
4	3	16.7
5	2	11.1
6	1	5.6
10	2	11.1
Total	18	100

towards universal banking and the resultant need to rapidly build multi-purpose banks providing commercial, investment and assurance services through a mix of acquisitions, mergers and strategic alliances.

It must be noted that by 1998 the concept of the universal bank in the UK was under question. The de-merger of BZW from Barclays Bank, of NatWest Markets from NatWest Bank and the increasing focus on specific products and markets by, for example, non-banking financial services providers such as Marks and Spencer, Tesco, Sainsbury's, Virgin and Internet banks such as Egg and Smile reflected this trend.

'How many of your strategic alliances are with partners in the following regions – Western Europe?'

A high (39) number of strategic alliances between UK and non-UK Western European banks and between Western European banks was noted as detailed in Table 4.3. The spread accorded with observations in Chapter Two whereby Western European banks tended to ally with a number of other Western European country banks to establish a cross-European network. This view is further supported by the range of one to five alliances seen with a valid percentage of over 12 per cent.

Table 4.3   Number of Partners in Western Europe

Number	Frequency	Percentage
1	12	30.7
2	5	12.8
3	6	15.4
4	5	12.8
5	7	17.9
6	1	2.6
7	1	2.6
11	1	2.6
19	1	2.6
Total	39	100

Table 4.4   Number of Partners in Eastern Europe

Number	Frequency	Percentage
1	4	57.1
2	1	14.3
3	1	14.3
4	1	14.3
Total	7	100

Table 4.5   Number of Partners in North America

Number	Frequency	Percentage
1	11	73.3
2	2	13.3
3	1	6.7
4	1	6.7
Total	15	100

'How many of your strategic alliances are with partners in the following regions – Eastern Europe?'

The number of alliances in Eastern Europe, as detailed in Table 4.4, was much lower (seven) than in Western Europe. In addition, the tendency to have more than one alliance was also markedly lower. This may reflect a number of issues, such as a possible perceived low relative importance of Eastern Europe (versus Western Europe) as a new market, the more recent nature of access and the economic re-adjustment problems of the region, the concentration of needs in the investment banking (privatization, consolidation, securities) areas rather than retail and a tendency to retain control, for example, through own branches rather than through alliances.

'How many of your strategic alliances are with partners in the following regions – North America?'

The 73.3 per cent concentration on one North American alliance, see Table 4.5, accorded with the trends observed in Chapter Two where a

Table 4.6   Number of Partners in Asia

Number	Frequency	Percentage
1	4	44.5
2	2	22.2
3	2	22.2
5	1	11.1
Total	9	100

typical cross-border alliance consisted of a number of Western European banks and one US bank. This linking with US banks may be due to the status of New York as a major world financial centre.

'How many of your strategic alliances are with partners in the following regions – Asia?'

The growth in the Asian Tiger economies over the 1980s and most of the 1990s period probably underlies the popularity of alliances with banks in this region as detailed in Table 4.6.

'How many of your strategic alliances are with partners in the following regions – Indian Sub-Continent, South and Central America, Africa, Middle East?'

Western European banks show only a limited tendency to enter into strategic alliances with partners in the regions of the Indian Sub-Continent, South and Central America, Africa and the Middle East. This may reflect the greater tendency to assert control in these regions through acquisitions (for example, Spanish banks acquiring Latin American banks) or having established branch networks dating from colonial days (for example, UK's Standard Chartered Bank).

Underpinning a strategic alliance is the understanding that member firms have access to accurate information about the financial condition of the members (reliable and audited annual reports), that there is a degree of symmetry in management style and that in the case of mishap, there is rapid, and unbiased, recourse to the courts to resolve disputes. In the case of non-Europe/US geographical areas, these under-pinning conditions may be considered to be (variably) lacking by potential firms considering alliances. Therefore the tendency may be to enter through one's own operations, such as representative offices and branches, where the firm can exert direct control over decisions and processes, rather than through arms length strategic alliances.

Future plans for strategic alliances

This section of the questionnaire asked respondents to provide information about future planned or possible geographical distribution of strategic alliance partners. A number of banks refused to complete this section, presumably because of competitive issues, in spite of assurances as to the maintenance of confidentiality.

A total of 68 responses were possible. They were asked to respond to:

'We are using or intend to use strategic alliances to expand our capability in – UK'

A high percentage of 55.2 per cent said they are using alliances and 26.3 per cent would consider further use of alliances with UK banks as reported in Table 4.7. This latter group may have been laggards in entering into alliances who are now expanding their range of alliances or they may be experienced firms that have found alliances beneficial and intend to expand their range. The 34.2 per cent of those who responded 'no and no future plans' may be banks that restrict their operations to a particular geographical area (the German Landesbanken are an example) or they may have existing non-alliance operations in the UK. The final category, ('no and possible future plans' (10.6 per cent)) may refer to those who prefer a high degree of control rather than the looser control of a strategic alliance. Alternatively they may prefer to have the concept of alliances 'proved' prior to using it.

Table 4.7   Expansion Intentions in UK

Response	Frequency	Percentage
Yes but no further plans	11	28.9
Yes and possible future plans	10	26.3
No and no future plans	13	34.2
No and possible future plans	4	10.6
Total	38	100

Table 4.8   Expansion Intentions in Western Europe

Response	Frequency	Percentage
Yes but no further plans	9	16.1
Yes and possible future plans	32	57.1
No and no future plans	6	10.7
No and possible future plans	9	16.1
Total	56	100

In addition, many Western European banks will also have representative office, branch or subsidiary operations in the City of London due to its position as a global financial centre. The resulting need to establish alliances will be less in terms of cross-border types, because of the ability to use own branch; but intra-country, product or service specific alliances may be more prevalent.

'We are using or intend to use strategic alliances to expand our capability in – Western Europe'

The high positive response, 'yes and possible future plans' (57.1 per cent), may be due to changes in mechanisms underpinning the countries of the European Union and the resulting opportunities that have arisen. The responses are contained in Table 4.8. These changes include, for example, the harmonization of bank regulation allowing a bank licensed in one EU country to operate in another EU country without obtaining a further licence.

'We are using or intend to use strategic alliances to expand our capability in – Eastern Europe'

The high negative response 'no and no future plans' (41.2 per cent) probably indicates the high uncertainty of Eastern Europe in terms of ownership of property, the ability to auction and realize assets via the courts and the transition status of the economic system. Table 4.9 details the responses. All of these tend to push foreign banks towards the retention of control over their operations via branches or representative offices rather than through strategic alliances. In cases where banks (BNP/Dresdner, for example) have entered into alliances with local partners, these have been of the more tangible joint venture

Table 4.9   Expansion Intentions in Eastern Europe

Response	Frequency	Percentage
Yes but no further plans	1	2.9
Yes and possible future plans	9	26.5
No and no future plans	14	41.2
No and possible future plans	10	29.4
Total	34	100

Table 4.10   Expansion Intentions in North America

Response	Frequency	Percentage
Yes but no further plans	7	20.6
Yes and possible future plans	5	14.7
No and no future plans	15	44.1
No and possible future plans	7	20.6
Total	34	100

Table 4.11   Expansion Intentions in Asia

Response	Frequency	Percentage
Yes but no further plans	4	11.8
Yes and possible future plans	6	17.6
No and no future plans	15	44.1
No and possible future plans	9	26.5
Total	34	100

variety. The response 'no and possible future plans' (29.4 per cent) probably points towards the realization that countries of Eastern Europe are in transition and that opportunities are arising. Banks that responded thus are probably cautious but may be waiting for the right opportunity to present itself.

'We are using or intend to use strategic alliances to expand our capability in – North America'

As noted earlier, North America, and particularly New York, is a prime world financial centre where most banks will already have substantive direct, alliance or at least correspondent bank relationships. The minority may wish to upgrade the latter. Table 4.10 details these responses.

'We are using or intend to use strategic alliances to expand our capability in – Asia'

Asia, as noted earlier, continues to be an area where Western European bankers wish to establish alliances. Table 4.11 details these responses.

'We are using or intend to use strategic alliances to expand our capability in – Indian Sub-Continent, South and Central America, Africa, Middle East'

The very high negative responses to the possibility of future expansion via the strategic alliance route in the Indian Sub-Continent, South and Central America, Africa and Middle East regions may be due to:

i)   the issue of control by the parent firm of operations in areas where the 'rule of law' is not strong or where the markets are not information transparent.
ii) the focus of the respondents, large Western European banks, on the opportunities generated by the EU in Western Europe and by the collapse of the Berlin Wall in Eastern Europe.

Additional observations

At the end of the questionnaire respondents were asked for any observations that they considered important. These responses ranged from short sentences to a comprehensive two-page response.

A British bank stated that it 'has entered into several other strategic alliances in the past, but the relationship has been terminated when the benefit has been achieved and no further value was to be gained'. This accords with the view that the strategic intent of the firm drives its actions, the firm identifies certain needs (defensive or offensive, access to tangible or intangible resources, access to products or markets) and makes the decision to fulfil these needs via a strategic alliance. The continuation of the strategic alliance is predicated on the continuation of benefits to its members.

A second British bank noted that 'strategic alliances are becoming increasingly critical – particularly due to IT and Communications – all enablers of reduced geographical constraints'. Opportunities to expand the geographical spread of countries in which the bank can offer its products and services lead to the need to access specialized knowledge of the foreign market through a cross-border 'link', often enabled via a strategic alliance.

A British cooperative bank stated 'It is difficult to be accurate in filling in this survey. Within a group like ... there are many relationships and no one person is familiar with all of them, how they work, what the objectives are and so on. I have tried to give a sense of how we look at things ...'. This response provides an insight into the link between an individual intra-firm strategic intents and the resulting alliance. Any particular firm may have a number of diverse strategic intents, located at different places in the firm, that are realized through a diverse set of inter-firm strategic alliances.

A German commercial bank noted that it has two types of alliances. The first type relates to three alliances with insurance companies to provide brokerage on a domestic scale in three different geographical areas. This is a product specific, geographically bounded strategic alliance. The second is a broad-based, global alliance 'together with an outstanding foreign banking group, concerning all third countries' activities'. A firm can enter into alliances to simultaneously serve a number of objectives, domestic and international.

A Luxembourg based bank drew attention to two alliances: one a product and knowledge capital based fund management operation and the other a co-location of its bank offices. The bank could use alliances as a mechanism to facilitate its operations in any area it saw fit. The configuration and purpose of the alliances can vary substantially.

A Norwegian bank proposed three categories of the strategic alliances that it had entered into: structural, product, and infrastructure.

Structural – A number of Scandinavian banks entered into a strategic alliance with the explicit intent that, over a pre-envisioned time, members would ultimately merge to form a regional champion. Here it was intended that convergent co-evolution, leading to a merger, would take place. Due to a change in the external context (a regional banking crisis), differential divergent co-evolution took place and the alliance was disbanded.

Product – The initial strategic intent, between the bank and an insurer, was convergent co-evolution leading towards merger. The reality was differential parallel co-evolution leading to the disbanding of the alliance and finally the acquisition of the insurer by the bank.

Infrastructure – A number of Norwegian banks have cooperated in establishing infrastructure alliances that serve the interests of all banks. However, the cost of these alliances has been borne by the larger banks that may now seek to establish their own restricted membership alliances.

The foregoing display the broad range of strategic intents that are served by various forms of strategic alliances and show that intents may change over time.

Conclusion

This chapter reports the responses of 44 questions contained in the questionnaire. The purpose of the questionnaire was to broadly survey the proclivities of senior managers in large European banks with regard to strategic alliances.

In the academic context the strategic alliance, cooperation agreement, collaborative arrangements, joint venture and so on, have a variety of meanings and integral assumptions. At the start of this research a definition of strategic alliance was developed from first principles, and this definition was embedded in the research. In the first section of the questionnaire the respondents were asked to comment on the validity of the consistent parts of the definition. The majority agreed that durability, the sharing or pooling of resources, a mechanism, strategic importance to partners, mutual and own firm economic gain were all elements of a strategic alliance.

Respondents were asked how important they considered a number of reasons for entering into a strategic alliance. There was support for the sharing of risks, entering a new product or geographical market reasons for entering into alliances. Reduction in the cost of capital is generally considered to be an important reason for entering into strategic alliances in most industries – but this was not so in this survey with regard to the European banking sector.

A number of questions regarding the formation of alliances were asked. The majority had a small, rather than large, number of alliances, were willing to enter into alliances with their competitors and held that there was a direct relationship between ownership and control.

With regard to managing these relationships, the majority reported that their alliances have met or are meeting strategic objectives, that these objectives are specific and underpinned by specific tasks. A degree of calculated initiative in pursuit of these objectives and tasks was allowed. The degree of commitment was high, and time was spent in agreeing to methods of making decisions.

As the strategic intents of the members of the alliance change, so the alliance needs to evolve, as discussed at the start of this chapter and detailed in Chapter Five. Respondents stated that substantial time was taken at the start of an alliance to establish methods for monitoring the implementation of decisions and resolving conflicts. The main focus of alliance activity among the respondents was clearly on Western Europe, and this pattern was repeated with regard to future alliance activity.

Questionnaire based surveys generally have, at their core, an attempt to gain a view of the consensus with regard to the particular issue or issues being addressed. The purpose of the questionnaire and its place in this research is to broadly identify the proclivities of strategic managers in large European banks with regard to strategic alliances.

In addition the responses have engendered a debate in the previous pages about the complexity of the issues addressed and provided a partial answer to the question – Do strategic alliances add value?

Clearly they do but the tendency is to use alliances in a particular geographical and legal context – Europe, North America – rather than continents – Africa, Latin America – where property rights are not so clearly defined and defensible. Alliances were entered into where useful and disbanded as their use declined.

Chapter Five provides further insights regarding the use of alliances through reporting the analysis of the semi-structured interviews.

5
The Substance of Alliances

Introduction

Key substantive issues can only be explored by dialogue with senior organizational members who are or have been prime movers in the strategic alliance and can therefore provide insights, from the inside, on the causes, effects and major processes relevant to the establishment, development and dissolution of the alliances.

This chapter is based on the interviews conducted with twenty-four senior managers, main board members or head office executives, in nine European countries. The interviews were conducted using a number of semi-structured thematic questions, as detailed in Appendix 1. The insights gleaned are reported below under the broad themes of background, conceiving cooperation, forming cooperation, organizing cooperation, evolving cooperation and dissolving cooperation which we identified as key issues in the review of the academic literature in Chapter Three.

Background

The external context typically establishes the conditions necessary for strategic alliances to be considered as an appropriate form of business organization. Many examples of this relationship can be seen. Let us give two particular examples – OPEC in the 1970s and the EU in the 1980 and early 1990s:

When OPEC (the Organization of Oil Producing Countries) substantially increased the price of crude oil in the 1970s the flow of surplus funds, deposited in London by the oil producing countries and lent on to the oil consuming countries, led (in conjunction with other factors detailed in Chapter Two) to the establishment of the Euromoney markets centred in London. To access these markets a number of strategic alliances – clubs and consortium banks – were established with, largely, USA, UK and European participation. The C and CBs (also analyzed in Chapter Two of this book) lasted only as long as the underlying business rationale lasted. As this rationale ended alternative forms – foreign banks' own branches being established in London to access the Euromoney markets directly – became the norm.

An outcome of the establishment of the European Union (and the free trade in goods, services and labour) was to allow European banks to provide their products and services in a foreign European country. This process started through cross-European strategic alliances that allowed one bank's products and services to be distributed through the network and to the customers of another bank. As the business flow increased, own branch operations became more prevalent and more complex relationships developed.

In both of the above cases the strategic alliance was used as an organization form and method which allowed the members to test out a potential business stream – enabled through largely market (in the former) and largely regulatory (in the latter) changes in the context – to establish its continuity. This was carried out while sharing the cost and risk through a low commitment of tangible and intangible resources.

A bank's strategic alliances strategy is externally driven by a combination of political and economic developments (the move towards monetary union and greater economic integration) and client needs (greater cross-border activity by both industrial/commercial and financial clienteles).

The context is confirmed as an important issue in the interviews conducted.

Regulatory changes

In a number of instances a change in regulation at an international, national, industry or product level led to new business opportunities which then allowed the choice to use strategic alliances if thought appropriate.

The UK went through a process of deregulation and liberalization (starting during the 1980s) which reduced the barriers to foreign banks entering into London; allowed the establishment of Universal Banks; allowed mutual financial organizations to provide consumer loans and also allowed non-financial service organizations to provide consumer financial services. Alongside this was a greater re-regulation of the quality of information about products and a transparency of charges provided to the consumer as a foundation on which to exercise their free choice.

As British banks decided to provide new products for the domestic consumer they established clearly defined strategic alliances (with an inbuilt implicit or explicit finite life) with the agenda to provide these products (in the short term) and to internalize know-how about how to produce, package, market and manage such products themselves in the future. Examples include:

- Alliances between banks and general insurance and life assurance companies to provide and all the banks to internalize know-how gained from the insurance companies with a later go-it-alone strategy being employed by some of the banks.
- Mutual organizations authorized to provide consumer loans established alliances with loan companies and gained access to the latter's credit-scoring systems.

The above general examples are supplemented by a host of specific intra-country alliances established to provide product and services in a more efficient way by using specialized providers who worked in a complementary way. In one example a major Bureau de Change operation took over the running of this service in the branches of a bank, thereby allowing the bank to outsource foreign currency and travellers cheques handling but retaining its own branding and location; in another the demand for national coverage in a sparsely populated large country led to an alliance with the Post Office accessing the extensive office network; in another case the EFTA/EU agreement allowed liberalization but government maintained a 'golden share' in the national banks to stop takeovers which in turn led to an increased use of alliances; in another case national (home country) restrictions on the bank's ability to operate overseas branches may have led to a greater use of alliances.

Market changes

As the Euromoney markets have developed into a global financial system with global linkages the propensity to seek business opportunities on a global scale has increased. The principles of complementarity, as seen in intra-country alliances is also at the core in international alliances and is used to capture a perceived business stream. Some alliances are set up in a strategic way (for example to access Eastern Europe), others in a more opportunistic and experimental way (to access a specific business opportunity).

In the international arena strategic alliances are used to:

- Access the foreign partners' distribution network (branches) and market products prevalent in one country to consumers in the other country where the product would be considered new.
- To produce a new activity, for example, British private-equity know-how into Australia; British and New Zealand fund management of Indian HNWI funds; British investment into private companies in Japan; Global investment expertise for variously located retail funds.

Alliances allow the ability to enter into new product or geographical markets quickly as opportunities arise and to re-configure as these opportunities change.

Technology changes

The Coase (1937) conception of the firm (as analyzed in Chapter One) was of closed boundaries within which the manager-entrepreneur undertook a number of activities that collectively added up to the business being conducted. The firm internalized – typically – inbound logistics, production, outbound logistics, marketing, servicing and support activities (human resources, finance and so on) – and went into the market place to gather resources or to access customers. The parts of the firm were located in one place or in a number of places (with access through physical transport links to each other) that – critically – were all under the control of the manger-entrepreneur in terms of direction, activity, employees and the security and control of information, physical products and other parties access.

Technology – the personal computer and the internet – enables parts of the 'firm' to be located far from each other and yet still communicate without time lags. The nature of the Coasian firm is the same as the 1937 conception in that the manager-entrepreneur remains in control of direction and resources but it has changed in that the resources may be located a long way away or may belong to another firm but be 'rented' through contracts by the firm under analysis.

A non-financial services sector virtual bank can now own the marketing relationship, deliver the products electronically (alongside retail, post and agency sales networks) and outsource much of its activities – for example IT to IBM, HR to Hayes, Finance and Credit Control to a bank. The boundaries of the virtual bank (firm) now extend to the parts of the partner organization, wherever located, that are allocated by contract to this virtual bank. The security and control of data becomes paramount and the boundaries of the firm become increasingly contractual and virtual or electronic. Examples of this process include infrastructure alliances such as DELTA and ATMs and virtual banks such as Sainsburys Bank, Egg, Intelligent Finance *et al.*

The developments in technology provide new opportunities for banks. Some make the high investment to gain the advantage of being first, others wait until the service is proven before providing the same. Technology reduces the boundaries between products, increases the need for scale (to off-set the costs of technology), changes the boundaries and leads to a more focussed industry and an exchange of skills through contracts.

Conceiving cooperation

Changes in the regulatory, market or technological contexts provide new opportunities for bankers to develop new streams of business and profit. The decision to enter into a particular product or geographical area is taken alongside the decision on the most suitable method of entry. So why are strategic alliances chosen?

Context

Context is clearly the key determiner of the decision to use a form of strategic alliance to meet business needs. This context can be at a number of levels from international to organizational.

On the international level this can be because of the globalization of financial services predicated on a desire to cross-borders in the pursuit of new products, markets and customers. In the interviews a number of examples pointed to the importance of the context:

- History and Geography – A Spanish bank wanted to internationalize but saw its core strength as building a bridge between Europe and Spanish speaking Latin America. The longstanding historical and linguistic link underpinned the ability to service trade and investment flows and to provide this ability to others. Later this strategy would lead to acquisitions by Spanish banks of local banks in Latin America.

- Regional Champions – At an IMF/World Bank meeting in 1984 four major Nordic banks, who knew each other from a consortium bank co-involvement in the 1970s, decided to consider the development of a strategic alliance as a precursor to merger. The reason for its foundation was the perceived need to establish a Scandinavian Champion to operate in the increasingly globally competitive environment. It was backed by strong top-level commitment and maintained through annual Salmon fishing expeditions between the top teams and their families.
- Primary Interests – A German bank whose major concern was financing, and gaining branch and customer networks in the newly open East Germany decided to place its international expansion in the hands of a strategic alliance, the most successful part of which was equity joint ventures in Eastern Europe.
- Focus – A Californian bank disposed of its international operations and focussed on the provision of credit in the home market thereby increasing credit quality. An alliance with a British global bank precluded poaching by other local banks with an international network by providing International Services for the former's customers and a Californian presence for the latter.
- Various Factors – A host of other contexts and contextual changes drive alliance activity. Internal policies and procedures preclude alliances; distinctive strengths – for example fisheries financing – determine the degree of geographical growth; Government policy precludes foreign ownership of local banks to maintain national integrity or precludes the opening of some types of foreign branches; differences in personal tax regimes predispose people to live in one European country and work in another and therefore provide an opportunity for the offer of new products.

The contexts are as varied as the number of countries, banks and customer needs. In some cases the context – a prohibition on the establishment of certain types of branches by Swiss Banks outside Switzerland – determines that strategic alliances must be used. In other cases – the decision to establish eventually a Scandinavian Regional Champion – led to a choice in favour of a strategic alliance between national banks, which over time would build relationship, technology and process links leading to convergence and merger.

Issues

When determining whether to enter into a strategic alliance, rather than some other form of business organization, issues to consider are varied. As mentioned above some decisions may be predetermined by national legislation, but in most cases the potential entrants into the alliance may chose between organic growth, strategic alliances and mergers and acquisition routes to achieve expanding capability. What then are the key issues to consider in deciding (where the choice is available) on the alliance as the preferred form?

The interviews pointed to a broad range of reasons:

- Opportunistic – As opportunities arose to gain 'economic benefit', (a realization that may well be at business group level that) the strategic alliance allows a quick reaction to capture these opportunities without an excessive commitment of resources or contracts. An additional benefit is that the alliance is also relatively easy to terminate. Alliances may provide joint opportunities, a synergy of fit, opportunity to enter a new market, or opportunity for a partner to learn about a new sector of their domestic market.
- Legal restrictions – Some countries stop the acquisition of local banks either through formal barriers or through informal barriers. Others allow internal alliances – such as between a bank and the national post office branches – rather than an acquisition so as to maintain a diverse provision.
- Sharing expertise – The alliance form allows firms that are not in the same industry to share their expertise to achieve a common goal. An example is of a 'Fastbox' outlet located in Switzerland which was built through an alliance between a kiosk retailer of cigarettes/ newspapers/chocolate, an IT firm, a bank and, a provider of tickets for entertainment. Individually none of the partners would consider acquiring the other and entering into their industry. Collectively, via a strategic alliance, they can configure the service and all gain additional customers and revenue.
- Infrastructure needs – Banking requires a set of infrastructure alliances (See Chapter Six for a discussion) that underpin and enable banking activity. Infrastructure alliances include clearing systems (BACS); electronic point of sale systems (SWITCH, DELTA); retail payment systems (VISA); automated teller machines (ATMs) and funds transfer systems (IBOS, SWIFT). The majority of banks need these services and membership is very broad thereby spreading the cost.
- Country conditions – Even where there are no formal barriers to entering a country through a strategic alliance, the nature of local conditions may preclude this choice. Clear and determinable property rights, backed up by a legal system based on proof rather than

personal preference, is necessary to allow the firms in an alliance to establish and terminate contracts. Without this the only mechanism for control would be through direct ownership of the overseas firm and direction of its employees. Banks showed a tendency to enter into countries through strategic alliances where clear (tangible and intangible) property rights are possible and show a great reluctance to enter into countries through strategic alliances where property rights are not clear.

- Organizational conditions – In some internal contexts an assignment to a strategic alliance may be considered a move out of the mainstream career path and may not attract candidates or have due importance in the partner firm's psyches. Particular banks have certain internal ethos – Co-operative Bank for example – that predispose them to enter into alliances only with those banks that have a similar internal ethos.

The decision on whether to enter into a strategic alliance, as opposed to some other form, is dependent on the objectives, special considerations (as analyzed above) and the likelihood, as judged by the prospective partners, of the alliance being successful.

Success

A number of factors are identified as pointers toward a successful strategic alliance. A Swiss bank was clear in its review of these factors:

- a similar customer base in the retail or medium sized business area,
- the bank's existing regional structure was used. Regional managers initiated and were the focus of co-operation in the region,
- strategic decisions on co-operation were taken at the Head Office,
- implementation of the operations was considered most important,
- customer lines were managed though the Key Accounts System,
- the relationship manager must be able to see a direct benefit of an alliance in servicing their customers' needs.

This clear menu was supported by a British bank which found partners which displayed a 'similar strategy, or similar perception of the external circumstances, a similar uncertainty about how to respond to it, similar difficulties I suppose in terms of resources ... and a focus on SMEs ... and a similar culture'.

A heavy focus on implementation was seen as a determinant of success. In IT outsourcing the long term planning horizon (three-five years), the heavy unionization of the industry and the serious implications for the business if projects were not properly completed made accurate and timely implementation critical. In another case the build up, over a long time (over 70 years in one example), of relationships (which delivered good products and cleanly resolved difficulties) between a retail bank and professional workers' affinity groups, led to a great degree of customer loyalty and to the identification of the bank with the affinity groups and the customer sector.

Continued use

A number of research findings pointed to the continued use of alliances. A British bank's core activity is to provide retail financial services to members of professional workers' affinity group. At establishment it provided insurance services to an affinity group. Now this bank provides a range of services to a number of such groups. Its customer acquisition and distribution method are the same, the affinity group, with both parties gaining from the relationship. So, in this case, the alliance strategy is a core part of the business model and will continue to be used.

While the reasons for entering into alliances are known, it was noted that the decision to enter into an alliance with a particular firm in a particular market could lead to other non-alliance member banks not dealing with the alliance partners as a self-protective measure.

Forming cooperation

Once the decision to use a strategic alliance as the mechanism for meeting identified business needs is made, the next issue is how to form this collaboration. The literature identifies three main issues for consideration.

Core processes

Researchers point to the core processes inherent in a strategic alliance. These processes include those to do with finance, control, learning and strategy.

With regard to finance a German bank in the sample was clear that an increase in shareholder capital to fund international expansion would be negatively correlated with the value of the shares to shareholders. So this bank tended to use methods of expansion that limited the use of expensive bank capital – equity joint ventures, contractual alliances – all of which include sharing the financial costs.

The control issues were often noted. Alliances allow a 'risk sharing' that can include the reduction of risk by co-opting local know-how thereby reducing the 'likelihood of problems'. It is clear, however, that this also leads to more tenuous control – as control is dispersed over a wider range of people in two or more firms. How do banks deal with these issues?

Again a German bank used the equity joint venture form of alliance, establishing a separate company with its own independent Board and management structure, so that there is 'respect for local necessities' with minimal interference from the head quarters of the parent companies. Developing this idea, a number of British banks started from the premise that 'relationships' were most important – that alliances were formed and based on goodwill, trust, mutual understanding and later underpinned by contracts, joint ventures, policies, rules, regulations. Serving and delivering the mutual interest was the core activity of the alliance. In one case a clear preference was for independent action, with a cultural bias against sharing, and a strong desire to maintain control.

In many cases, particularly German and British banks, managers noted the importance of learning. Alliances may be initiated by a 'regulatory impulse', an identified specific opportunity, and the parallel identification of the lack of knowledge in an area required to deliver the benefits of the opportunity. Banks sought alliances with partners who could bring 'greater experience and greater strength' in the required area. Alliances developed from a 'smaller nucleus' then grew as the rationale grew.

The parallel or convergent nature of the strategies of the firms considering entering into an alliance was very important. A Dutch bank was clear that the strategy of cross-border alliances to access the other partner's home country branch networks, and to increase the distribution network, was flawed. Rather they chose to specialize in developing an expertise, emerging markets, which they subsequently provided to all.

Cultural dissimilarity

International alliances add the dimension of cultural dissimilarity. A British bank reflected on its three small local alliances in Spain, France and Italy that were designed to gain local expertise and to try out a new market. The alliances failed to deliver and were disbanded. What were the reasons?

- 'it's very difficult for financial services organisations to cross national boundaries',

- 'you have to get it right between imposing your culture and your product offering into that market'.

The cultural dimension manifests itself in a number of areas such as national characteristics (however defined), business ethos, nature of agreements, even language used. On the more practical front, international systems such as VISA, MasterCard and SWIFT allow a degree of operational homogeneity between banks which in many respects are dissimilar. The local currency cheque clearing systems, by and large, designed for local needs, and time consuming collection systems often end up being used for foreign cheques. IT systems may not be compatible and may require major investment to underpin the alliance.

A number of those interviewed pointed to some form of pre-existing relationship with an overseas bank or foreign country. This relationship, and resultant mutual understanding, was the underpinning of successful alliances. A Spanish bank mentioned, on the one hand, its linguistic and trade links with some parts of Latin America, and on the other the trade and political links with the rest of Europe. This put it in a unique position to act as a 'financial services bridge' between Europe and Latin America.

Cultural fit is used as a term to describe a 'meeting of minds', the latter a phrase that encompasses a number of issues including:

- a view of the world that is in harmony – for example: co-operative banks sharing an ideology,
- a parallel or convergent understanding of the key opportunities in Europe, or in a product market,
- a mutual understanding and respect on a very human level (a personal 'resonance'.

As one British banker said:

'if you get along with people you are more likely to achieve things faster and again you have to be able to, I hesitate to say the ..., share a vision ..., but I think it means really sharing perhaps a cultural fit, sharing a view of the market where it's going, and seeing how that can go.'

It could be said that a successful cross-border strategic alliance is one where cultural fit is high. However it may be that the best arrangement is when cultural fit in managerial processes and world-view is high (so the partners can work together), but cultural dissimilarity in product or geographical knowledge for example is also high so that there is the possibility to learn from the partner.

Thus:

Cultural Fit (managerial processes + world-view) + Cultural Dissimilarity (product or geographical knowledge) = mutually beneficial and valuable knowledge transfer = successful strategic alliance.

Decision-making

Within an alliance a variety of decision-making mechanisms can be identified. These mechanisms are driven both by the nature of the business and the managerial ethos.

In the case of an investment fund alliance between British and Japanese partners the process started with a feasibility study which led to a structure that is standard in the industry – a partnership agreement with a pre-determined life to invest, gain return and dissolve. The relationship between the two parent companies is encapsulated in a management company that runs the various investment fund companies.

This industry determined arrangement is very different from a British bank that set its own clear agenda when managing alliances. The decisions to enter into alliances between two or more banks are based on strategic thinking at Group level. Once the decision had been made the management of the functional alliance (or the functional parts of a broader alliance) were considered:

> 'very specific to subsidiaries, or operational areas and therefore the authority to manage them was delegated down to either the functional manager in the case of a technology alliance, or the chief executive of a subsidiary who is managing those alliances as a main part of his business.'

Once the decision has been made to enter into an alliance the possible internal and cross-partner structures are many fold.

A German bank, upon agreeing to collaborate with a partner, set up a joint venture vehicle and a business plan approved by the head quarters of the parent banks. The preferred method was to appoint joint venture managing directors, one from each parent, who ran a largely self-contained and self-directed joint venture.

Various ongoing processes were used to facilitate the operations of the alliance and to engender closer cooperation. These ranged from a 10 year planning horizon (British bank); specialist two-three person committee to prepare the 'grand vision' (Norwegian bank); a reciprocal board membership and a small cross-shareholding (a French bank); person exchange programmes (a French and a German bank); a coming together for specific activities but also maintaining a clear separate identity (a German bank).

In designing products 'review meetings' were held (reported a British bank) where decisions were made on 'what kind of products are being offered'. It was clearly important in this case to match the alliance insurance partners' product design, business culture, and delivery to the needs of the banks customers.

A British bank stated that the levels of responsibility for lending, expenditure, contracts and so on are very clearly defined. However no one place is identified as responsible for joint ventures. In general the head of a department wishing to enter into an operations based alliance would ask the 'Executive Committee member responsible for a particular area ... [to take the time to] ... take a view as to whether he felt it was something that he needed to bring to the table ... [at the Executive Committee] ... to get the approval of his colleagues'. Any approved alliances may be based on a number of legal contracts which if required will be arranged by the legal department.

These alliances would be supported by time spent in building up a personal as well as a professional relationship. Accordingly 'so we sponsor their rally cars, we play cricket against them each year, we go to their golf tournaments but more than that we report our numbers to them every month, actual numbers, profit and loss and number of customers.'

The decision-making mechanisms are in two main areas:

- deciding whether to enter into an alliance, with whom to enter into it, for what purpose and under what terms,
- once the decision has been made, how to structure and manage the collaboration,
- how to develop bonding and mutual respect between the partners managers and staff.

Organizing cooperation

Benefits and dangers

The organization and configuration of the alliance attempt to reap the benefits and mitigate the dangers. The benefits are identified by managers as being important, and therefore it is important to mitigate the danger of an alternative provider taking on this business. These dangers are often of a specific nature – geographically, organizationally or customer based.

A particularly clear example of this is the Swedish bank that built an alliance with the Swedish Post Office. The benefits (and mitigations) of this alliance were of three tiers:

- Geographically specific – the need to meet the regulatory require-ment to service customers all over the largely rural and widely dis-persed population. Entering into this alliance secured the network and excluded competitors.
- Organizational specific – The Swedish Post Office provided lower transaction costs as their customers carry out limited transactions.
- Customer specific – The network allows the servicing of customers throughout the country, allowing the gathering of low cost deposits and the selling of new products.

The definition of a customer varies – Swedish salaried employees often have their accounts opened for them by the employer. Thus banks target and build alliances with employer firms and once the current account and salary credits are captured savings and loan products follow to develop a profitable relationship. Another example is the acquisition of a branch in Copenhagen by a German bank that was predicated on the Germans bank's desire to build a competence centre starting from servicing the Baltic Sea business through to providing shipping finance. Alternatively, process decisions such as to reduce costs or increase effectiveness may be underpinning the decision to enter into a specific alliance.

Form complexity

Alliances are complex organizational forms. They range from high degrees of formality to high degrees of informality. A sample is provided below.

Formal forms include a Board based management team for a Joint Venture; a swap of board directors and an alternative or alternating chairman; Board decisions communicated to operational departments (and a dormant Steering Group); formalities due to legal structures and agreements with seamless management; 'objectives are specific, iden-tify specific tasks, take calculated initiatives'; 'consider there is a direct positive relationship between equity and managerial control'; dialogue at senior board level and permanent dialogue between operating departments; preferred equity joint ventures; 10 per cent ownership swap; full recognition of clear and focussed business objectives; formal Board meetings; alliances must not get too independent; international alliance is 'more planned, much more structured and more thought about and perhaps more importantly much more committed from the point of view of both parties'; mutual representation on Board of Governors dealing with strategic issues, steering group established at start disbanded and operational units for coordination substituted.

Informal forms include interchange of people; working with banks of a similar size (and similarities in decision making systems, time scales and so on); agreements that allow (but do not force) participation in each other's loans; committees are forbidden; 'who has the best knowledge about it, who do we talk to ... who works on the tasks that they have over there'; a personnel swap between two partners of the alliance; absence of share stakes or a legal entity is not seen as an inhibiting factor in any way; periodic brainstorming, *ad hoc* task force activities designed to identify market opportunities, personal accountability of senior international officers in making alliances work; meetings between functional staff from partners.

There are as many forms of alliances (an unlimited combination of formal and informal forms) as there are alliances themselves.

Trust building

Alliance partners deliberately build trust between their firms to facilitate a successful alliance. The trust building themes are twofold – sufficient structure to allow discussion and sufficient flexibility to allow open dialogue. As one British bank said:

> No token shareholding and the Minutes of a meeting start with 'this is what we want to do together, it was very vague, deliberately and there's been no piece of paper since. It's just informal contacts'.

Relationships at all levels were built on patience and interaction in developing products and providing services. Whilst there was general understanding between Boards of Directors and specific contracts with separate organizations, informal relationships were engendered by the emphasis on sending young specialists from the French and German partners to the other for socialization thereby learning each others systems and cultures and then sending them into a third country.

Trust between the bank and its customer is very important. A British bank has built long-term relationships, some as long as 70 years, with affinity groups. Members of these groups trust the group and in turn the group trusts the bank. The relationship between the bank, affinity group and the individual customer is one of experience, trust, integrity and reliability.

To summarize 'the most important thing is actually that we have partners in daily business on which we can rely' and 'as the relationship builds over time, the deeper trust and personal relationships, so you can work together better and better'.

International complexity

International collaborations bring increased managerial complexity. To enter into a new country (as in the case of the Franco/German collaboration) the view emerged that it was easier to develop a new operation (singly or jointly). This would mitigate the complexity and difficulty of building a common culture as well as electronic computer systems from two existing groups. Rather the new operation, though jointly owned, would build its own systems and a distinct, individual culture.

In establishing an East European joint venture the French and German banks brought with them their corporate clients. Local knowledge was important:

> you should know the third country, the local country [in East Europe], you should have knowledge of banking and of the business reasonings and behaviour etc.

The international dimension has repercussions in staffing. In a Franco/German alliance a French minority group 'who have limited economic opportunities in mainstream France' lived just near the border and were put to work in the German partner bank where they could 'work like a German worker'.

The decision to go overseas is driven by a number of factors:

> 'A geographical expansion of a British bank to follow business opportunities through purchasing a 100 branch Portuguese bank and through following large corporate clients who are attempting to capture new business streams.'

International operations may be enabled and delivered by branches, by international electronic payments systems, or by agreement with overseas, otherwise independent, branches.

Co-evolving cooperation

Sustaining collaboration

As an alliance is established there is alignment between the parent firms' objectives and the objectives of the alliance. Alliances require the commitment of a dynamic individual or group of individuals whose personal input leads to the alliance performing. All three levels, parent firms, alliance members and individuals, have to co-evolve. Co-evolution leads to a longer-term alliance if it is still in accord with the underlying business rationale and thereby greater security of revenue. Co-evolution is required at all levels from strategy to delivery and clear, but changing, objectives lead to the delivery of a clear and appropriate result.

Co-learning

As alliances evolve a number of dimensions come into play with co-learning, often referred to as the most important.

The primary requirements of co-learning in an alliance are 'recognition of an identity of interest' which continues over time, and an ability to exchange information, ideas and insights. However, information cannot flow freely in alliances 'because it's sensitive information. Those things [free information flow] will become more difficult to manage as banks, building societies or insurance companies broaden their structures, their markets and the intermingling will become more confused.' Sometimes the strategic alliance will bring specific knowledge and the partner bank will internalize it.

Despite the above proviso many of those interviewed gave importance to the human processes that led to successful alliances through co-learning. For example:

- 'Enormous value from having someone that you trust and can talk about strategy', as one CEO remarked (it is lonely at the top).
- That alliances relied on trust, cultural fit, interpersonal support, equal partnership, mutual respect, core desire to maintain the relationship at a professional and personal level, open and honest dialogue, and mutual understanding.

In their daily work the alliance partners used networks and relationships to persuade and develop consensus. This consensus changed as the strategic objectives changed and developed and the positive and negative experiences of alliances determined the nature, management and development of the next alliance.

Products were co-designed to meet specific needs, in response to specific events and client needs and this was carried out at an operational level. As one banker said 'a lot of time was put into the question to find out which way we can make more business together'.

Another bank enabled the product development process by holding meetings every four-six weeks to identify areas of mutual concern and interest based around encouragement and coaching rather than structures. These alliance partners try to be proactive in considering all areas of business through allowing ideas to spark and then try to develop them together.

International issues

Particular firms and countries display particular concerns. The main concern, with regard to the international context, was accessing the learning curve effects of the overseas location. Entering into alliances with overseas banks to access the overseas market allowed the internalization of the local business culture and mitigated against the perceived differences. A German co-operative bank attempted to further mitigate the national business culture 'issues' in Spain and Eastern Europe by building alliances solely with other co-operative banks, who had a similar 'co-operative ethos' overlaying their national business culture.

Dissolving cooperation

Ceasing rationales

A strategic alliance is usually established to satisfy a business need – to enter a new geographical or product market, to access new knowledge – and co-evolve as the strategic needs of their parent companies evolve.

Alliances are dissolved when they no longer serve the needs of all the partners. The method of dissolution may range from a total disbanding to an internalization by one partner of the activity-competence of the former alliance. In both cases the alliance has not in some way 'failed' but rather delivered what it could or was required to deliver and is no longer an appropriate way for the former partners to meet their business needs.

Again the reasons for dissolution may be as varied as the alliances dissolved. A sample of the observations made by interviewees on the subject of dissolving alliances is provided below ordered by the nationality of the bank(s) that made observations regarding the dissolution of the alliance.

In the case of British banks:

- 'one of the philosophies we have is shareholder return and by that it's not just mouthing the philosophy we actually try to make a decision based on it ... so you've got to be constantly planning and analysing what is it you're getting out of this ... what else can we do ... if it's a more balanced contract, then the other side should be thinking the same thing as well',
- dissolving an alliance is a considered decision as it has a direct impact on one's and one's partners business,
- agreements govern the access to underpinning technology so that if the alliance is dissolved then access to the technology will still continue,
- one British-Indian JV is being terminated 'because of the particular circumstances of the alliance and it has a natural life and that's really all [there is] to be said'. Documents regarding termination are 'substantially irrelevant in a sense that it's the fact that is important, and if there's nothing for the venture to do then the venture's life is limited and terminated',
- the reasons for termination depend entirely on the venture – it may be at the end of its natural life, a failed venture or have successfully carried out what it needs to do,
- they considered themselves ruthless about the tangibility of the alliance and equally ruthless about the non-viability of an alliance. Dissolving includes the issues of contracts, exit periods and so on. The viability of the alliance was checked via the financial planning process,

In the case of a Dutch Bank:

- it presumed a good fit between Dutch-Uruguay partners from a business point of view but suffered from a clash of cultures. The Dutch bank injected capital and management expertise but the local bank resisted the business plan developed so it pulled out. With hindsight it is important to 'talk fundamentals from the outset' to establish whether there is a meeting of minds between the prospective partners.

In the case of a German bank:

- the formal termination provision may be addressed in different ways. The statutes of the alliance include termination clauses. In Germany they use two-six pages to address all the issues rather than the Anglo-Saxon 60 plus pages.

In the case of a Norwegian bank:

- the alliance collapsed with worse relations than before except at the founding fathers/old chairman level. The gains of the 1980s – payments systems, multinational corporation subsidiary accounts – were lost. Because staving off the bankruptcy of the firm was more important than the alliance it became secondary, but could have been reactivated. The new managing directors and chairmen wanted to put blue-water between previous policies and current policies. The underlying Scandinavian consortium bank collapsed as well when the vision collapsed and practical operational initiatives started to fall to pieces. A financial crisis in the early 1990s led to a non-functioning alliance by 1992 and by 1995 all areas of the co-operation between the four banks terminated and the underlying vehicle dissolved. Now the former partners only have normal correspondent banking relationships,
- it set up an alliance with a Swedish bank in London but closed because the 'war aims' of the two partners diverged after the strategic alliance was formed. They had a specialized ship financing company, together with some other rich banks. The specialist company was taken over by one of the members and the joint venture with a Swedish bank closed down because branches wanted to become too independent.

In the case of a Spanish Bank:

- a former alliance with a bank in France, regarding mergers and acquisitions work, was cancelled after one and a half years due to problems with the business flow (from France into Spain rather than vice versa) and problems with letters of credit and so on. An agreement with the Italian bank in the leasing area was the local initiative of an Italian bank manager in Spain and dissolved when the manager moved on to other responsibilities.

In the case of a Swiss Bank:

- a failed alliance in Italy was credited to an inability to enter into cross shareholdings.

In the above we have deliberately cited a wide range of factors and causes concerning dissolution, often supported by quotations from the discussions, because that does represent the spread of testimonies offered by the respondents. There are, however, some themes present through these testimonies. First the alliance is measured against some criteria – profitability, tangibility, shareholder value, and found wanting. Second, cultural incompatibility is recognized *post factum*. Third, the alliance has run its course, served its purpose, or is no longer appropriate in changed circumstances.

Conclusion

The senior managers' core interests, as noted by the degree of discussion in each area, were the global, national and market context and the two areas of the conceiving and forming cooperation. The organizing and co-evolution areas received less attention in the discussions. This may be because, based on this review, these elements were dealt with in real time by non-Board levels of management and operational people and were not directly the responsibility of senior management, other then in setting policy. The dissolving cooperation question resulted in detailed responses with, in many cases, an expression of the lessons learnt.

The research material reported in Chapter Four generated valuable pan-European data enabling developments and trends in strategic alliance formation to be identified. The present chapter is complementary in that it explores the internal dynamics of strategic alliances in European banking. Substantive insights about the lifecycle of alliances, as seen from the inside by practicing senior managers, are reported and analyzed. We found here how the alliances commenced, what the participants thought – what the ensuing experience was.

The next chapter provides a final response to the question posed at the start of this book – 'Do Strategic Alliances Add Value?', revisits our understanding of strategic alliances and proposes two areas of further research – infrastructure alliances and the co-evolution of (strategic intents in) strategic alliance model.

6
Discussion, Infrastructure Alliances and Co-Evolution

Introduction

In this final chapter we seek to provide a response to the question 'Do Strategic Alliances Add Value?' as posed at the start, and a *leitmotiv* of the book. The definition of a strategic alliance as posited in Chapter One is revisited and revised. A summary of the contribution of this research to academic knowledge and the practice of alliances is provided. As a result of findings in this research, further research into the infrastructure alliance and into the co-evolution model is proposed together with some suggestions for a future research agenda.

Conclusion

Do strategic alliances add value?

The observed phenomena of an exponential increase in the use of strategic alliances was examined in this research using the epistemology of Transcendental Realism (Lawson, 1997) wherein scientific enquiry is aimed 'at identifying the underlying structures and mechanisms ...', a movement from the observed to the underlying. To investigate this movement from observed to underlying a number of scientific research tools were utilized.

We examined the research question through five types of analysis and at two levels of engagement – through an analysis of the strategic alliance from first principles (at firm level) based on the foundation work, 'The Nature of the Firm' by Coase (1937); through a 23 year historical review of secondary data (at industry level); through a review of over 400 papers in the academic literature (at firm and industry level); through a questionnaire survey of European banks (at firm level again) and through in-depth interviews of senior managers (also at firm level). This research examined the European banking industry.

As argued in Chapter One, Coase (1937) set out to explain the rationale of the firm that is, at the simplest, the existence of transaction costs and uncertainty ('bounded rationality') may make it less costly, less risky or both to internalize inherently separate economic activities within the boundaries of the firm. The strategic alliance was detailed in terms of its form, nature, purpose and importance and identified as taking an intermediate position on the continuum between market based, arm's length transactions on the one hand and relationships and hierarchic, or intra-firm transactions and relationships on the other. Glaister and Buckley (1994) identified a dichotomy between the purposes of market-based transactions and intra-firm transactions as reported in Figure 1.3. The strategic alliance allows one to balance the two extremes and therefore allow the firm to make more flexible choices, as available in the market, while at the same time securing the benefits of intra-firm operations.

The analysis of historical secondary data ranging over 23 years, as reported in Chapter Two, determined that the use of alliances went through three distinct lifecycles each of which, in different ways, added value to the alliance and member firms. The Clubs and Consortium Banks lifecycle (during the 1970s) enabled bankers located throughout Europe and the USA to internationalize (through, for example, a low commitment of capital, reduced risk, shared return and an easy potential exit) and to follow commercial opportunities whilst accessing the new established Euromarkets in London. Bankassurance (during the 1980s) allowed banks in the UK to take advantage of new opportunities afforded through the liberalization of the financial sector to provide various insurance services to bank customers, products and expertise being sourced through alliances with insurance companies. The Virtual Bank (starting during the 1990s and continuing) allowed the firms in Coase (1937) terms to disaggregate the firm through technology to disparate geographical locations and outsource to various providers whilst retaining control of the firm's operation and knowledge capital boundaries through contract based alliances. Virtual banks still exist as a viable method of organizing banking services. In all these cases – clubs and consortium banks, bankassurance and virtual banks – types of alliances add value in different ways as appropriate to the different context which they operate in.

The literature review in Chapter Three, shows quiet clearly that strategic alliances add value of different degrees, of different types and of different duration in a wide range of geographical, industry and firm contexts.

Our questionnaire survey of major European banks, as analyzed in Chapter Four, found that the reduction in the cost of capital, the sharing of risks, help in accessing product and geographical markets or distribution channels were all advantages gained through strategic alliances.

The analysis, reported in Chapter Five, of in-depth interviews with 24 senior managers across nine European countries has provided further insights into the alliance process and confirmed that alliances provide a number of benefits to the partners.

To summarize:

- Strategic alliances allow the ability to balance 'markets' and 'intra-firm transaction' extremes and enjoy flexible choices in increasingly dynamic markets.
- Clubs and Consortium Banks and Bankassurance lifecycles display the value of alliances in allowing an early entry into a business area with later commitment. Virtual banks allow disaggregation of the firm while retaining strategic intent over its (owned or contracted) resources.
- Strategic alliances add value of different degrees and of different duration in a wide range of geographical, industry and firm contexts.
- Strategic alliances allowed, variously, a reduction in the cost of capital, the sharing of risks, accessing knowledge capital and resources, help in accessing product or geographical markets and distribution channels.
- Senior Directors confirmed that strategic alliances provided a number of benefits to partners. These benefits were at differential rates, of varying duration, in different ways and of varied impact.

Based on the wide-ranging analysis in this research it is possible to assert with a high degree of confidence that strategic alliances do add value and increase the range of strategic options available to Senior Directors.

Revised understanding of a strategic alliance

In Chapter One an extensive analysis of the form, nature, purpose and importance, of strategic alliances, based on the ground breaking work of Coase (1937) and Williamson (1982, 1986), was carried out and the strategic alliance defined as:

> A durable relationship established between two or more independent firms, involving the sharing or pooling of resources to create a mechanism (corporate or otherwise) for undertaking a business activity or activities of strategic importance to one or more of the partners for their mutual economic advantage.
>
> ul-Haq et al (1996)

In the research reported in this book it emerged that strategic alliances only lasted as long as the strategic rationale lasted. As long as the alliance continued to deliver sufficient value to the partners to continue, the alliance did continue. However if the converse was true the alliance would be disbanded, for example, through gradual withdrawal, through sudden and terminal disbanding or through internalization by one or other partner of some key element in the alliance based cooperation. In some cases the strategic alliance had a defined period of life – either measured in time or in outcomes – before disbanding occurred.

Our research suggests that firms entering into alliances hold the explicit or implicit view that the alliance will only last as long as the strategic advantages are forthcoming. In some form the alliance partners '*anticipate*' that the alliance will be dissolved at some future date. Accordingly the definition offered at the start of this research should be amended to:

> *A relationship of anticipated durability* established between two or more independent firms, involving the sharing or pooling of resources to create a mechanism (corporate or otherwise) for undertaking a business activity or activities of strategic importance to one or more of the partners for their mutual economic advantage.

Underlining the often limited lifespan of alliances, however, does not detract from the range of alliance-based value explored in these pages.

Contribution to knowledge

This research has provided a contribution to our knowledge of alliances in a number of areas: dynamic-disequilibrium, the distinction between Strategic versus Infrastructure Alliances, the (Changing) Nature of the Firm, Directors Areas of Interest, Geographical Scope and Property Rights, and Implications for Other Industries.

Dynamic-disequilibrium

This research provides a detailed summary of the major academic work in line with the lifecycle of an alliance: conceiving, forming, organizing, evolving, dissolving cooperation. This summary will be valuable to academics researching in this area and to practitioners initiating and running alliances as it brings together the core findings in one accessible document.

The springboard we find is that deregulation, increased use of technology, enhanced and fickle customer expectations, increased merger and acquisition activity, reduction in protectionism, increased formation of trading blocks and global competition have undermined the old certainties within which firms could achieve a sustainable competitive advantage over a long period. Markets no longer tend towards an equilibrium position but are continuously in a state of 'dynamic-disequilibrium'. Strategic alliances provide an essential mechanism and as we have shown a flexible one for rapid and repeat re-configuration to meet the external and internal challenges.

Strategic versus infrastructure alliances

The original definition of strategic alliances as 'obligational-contractual relations' which are '... [A] durable relationship[s] established between two or more independent firms, involving the sharing or pooling of resources to create a mechanism (corporate or otherwise) for undertaking a business activity or activities of strategic importance to one or more of the partners for their mutual economic advantage'. Research led to modifying this definition to 'A relationship of anticipated durability ...'. Strategic alliances are found to be set up to add value to members.

As a development of the foregoing we identified the 'infrastructure alliance', as a former strategic alliance that has broadened its membership so that it no longer provides a competitive advantage to its members but rather becomes an 'industry wide base-line provision'. Non-membership of an infrastructure alliance garners a competitive disadvantage for non-members. Infrastructure alliances add value to the industry. Infrastructure alliances are multilateral, provide a commodity service, provide strategic disadvantage by exclusion, are more embedded in the industry, have greater self-sufficiency.

For academics this new distinction between the 'strategic' and the 'infrastructure' forms of alliances opens up a new field of research as suggested in the section on Infrastructure Alliances below. Practitioners may use this classification to determine value chain modifying activities (through the strategic form) and industry dynamic modifying activities (through the infrastructure form). Some may focus on providing the industry underpinnings by deliberately forming and developing infrastructure alliances, leading to extraordinary profits for the founding shareholders as membership broadens and transaction volume increases.

The nature of the firm

We found evidence of 'obligational-contractual relations' underpinning all banking activity and considered them to be integral and essential and therefore posited a high industry specific 'propensity to cooperate'.

We discovered that Bankers follow income streams generated by customers. New income streams lead to bankers using alliances (1970s, 1980s) to service clients cautiously until the security of the income stream warrants direct investment. Furthermore we assert that the Coase (1937) conception of a firm as an independent organization with discernible boundaries has been changed by technology. The 'virtual firm' with the imposition of strategic intent over a number of activities, many carried out in different physical locations and by third party providers, is possible and underpinned by a bundle of, largely explicit and some implicit, contracts. This development has also been facilitated by a variety of factors including deregulation, freer movement of people and capital, by internationalization generally, as well as by enhanced competition between companies leading to a desire to outsource non-core activities.

Again both academic and practitioner interest in the implications for large dominant firms in particular established industries subject to competition from a fast moving, disaggregated collection of individual knowledge entrepreneurs and professional advisers is likely to be high. The academic will wish to develop understanding while the practitioner interest is more likely to be about using the understanding offered here to protect their dominant position (in the case of large firms) or to create new markets (in the case of newer faster moving firms).

Directors areas of interest

We carried out an analysis of the perspectives of Directors in the major banks in Europe according to the conceiving, forming, organizing, evolving, dissolving cooperation lifecycle.

The senior directors' core interests, as noted by the degree of discussion in each area, were the global, national and market context and the two areas of conceiving and forming cooperation. The organizing and co-evolution areas received less attention in the discussions. This may be because, based on this analysis, these elements were dealt with in real-time by non-Board levels of management and by operational staff and were not directly the day-to-day responsibility of senior management, other than in setting policy. The dissolving cooperation question resulted in some detailed responses with, in many cases, an expression of the lessons learnt. This first finding leads us to confirm earlier writing asserting the upward, outward and forward orientation of senior management.

Academic and practitioner interest is likely to be aligned with great interest in how Senior Directors (making global, national, market context, conceiving and forming stages judgements and decisions) can ensure delivery through operational (including front end) staff, whilst subject to the co-evolution of the partners' strategic intent and the partners and alliances delivery capability.

Geographical scope and property rights

We found that strategic alliance activity was clearly restricted to Europe and the same pattern was repeated for future alliance activity. A clear disinclination to enter into alliances in certain continents or sub-continents (Africa, Latin America) where property rights are not so clearly defined or defensible was observable in the interviews whilst capital cost reduction was not considered to be of *major* importance in choosing the alliance route. It should be said that the willingness of Spanish banks to engage in Latin America, no doubt predicated on long standing linguistic and trade links, is a possible exception to this generalization.

Academics may be interested in investigating the optimal level of discernible and determinable property rights and access to capital required to make alliances a possible choice whilst practitioners may wish to define the levels of risk acceptable in undertaking alliances.

Contribution to other industries

It would be fair to suggest that there are three key findings that have application to other industries. The first is our notion of the possibly changed nature of the firm, where dispersed capabilities are backed by strategic intent. A non-banking example of disaggregation is the pharmaceutical industry with its strategic alliances and/or cooperation with biotechnology companies, together with outsourced activities, some cross-border. The second, though more tenuous, would be the strategic alliances versus infrastructure alliance distinction. This is clearly found in the world of IT, where for example, all web-sites have bought into

Google, where Google has become a core requirement for the internet to work. The third is the strategic alliance co-evolution model explored in a later section.

Further research

In these last pages we would like to anticipate the question: Does your research prompt suggestions for further research? We end with two lines of inquiry to offer food for thought.

Infrastructure alliances

Whilst substantial research exists regarding the strategic alliance, some of which is reported in Chapter Three, much less research has been carried out on the infrastructure alliance detailed in Chapter One.

Infrastructure alliances are a 'base line provision' that are fundamentally important to the provision of banking services and banks have a high pre-existing propensity to enter into infrastructure alliance. Given the importance of such alliances this may well be an area warranting further theoretical and applied research.

Research could examine areas such as:

- the forces driving a strategic alliance to become an infrastructure alliance,
- the degree of potential 'oscillation' between infrastructure and strategic forms,
- the diverse forces acting on the 'oscillation' process,
- the lifecycle of an infrastructure alliance,
- the value chain of an infrastructure alliance,
- the co-evolution of infrastructure alliances and the member firms (see Figure 6.1 for 'The Co-Evolution Model'),
- the divergence between the provision of financial products and the provision of cross-industry infrastructure to support these products,
- regional and global convergence in infrastructure alliances,
- obtaining and sustaining a competitive advantage in infrastructure alliances,
- capturing and retaining profitability in infrastructure alliances.

The co-evolution model

In the forgoing analysis the co-evolution of the alliance partner strategic intent, in a similar direction, was a prerequisite to the continuation of the alliance.

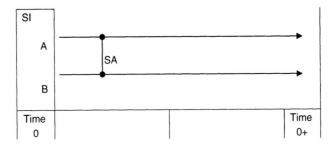

Parallel Co-Evolution

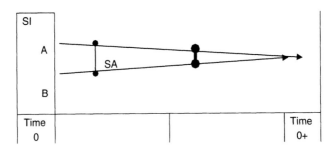

Convergent Co-Evolution

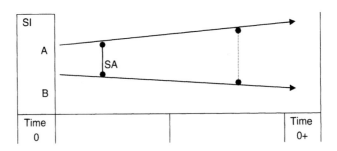

Divergent Co-Evolution

Key:

SI	=	Strategic Intent
SA	=	Strategic Alliance
A	=	Alliance Member A
B	=	Alliance Member B
Time 0	=	Time at Start of Alliance = Co-Alignment
Time 0+	=	Time in the Future

Figure 6.1 Schema for Classifying Co-Evolution of Firm Level Strategic Intents in Strategic Alliances

This co-evolution may be said to take three major forms – parallel co-evolution, convergent co-evolution, divergent co-evolution, see Figure 6.1.

Parallel Co-evolution – This is where the strategic intents of the two firms are evolving along paths that allow the continuation of the strategic alliance in the broad nature as at establishment. The initial matching of intents continues and evolves over time at the same rate, in a similar direction. Any *slight* changes in the speed of evolution of the individual intents of the member firms or in the degree of parallel evolution are compensated for by the 'springiness' or flexibility of the strategic alliance. If the degree of convergence or divergence in intents is too great and cannot be compensated for, then the following classifications apply.

Convergent Co-evolution – This is where the strategic intents of the two firms converge over time and the rationale behind the strategic alliance is strengthened. This strengthening may ultimately lead to the merger of the two firms and the 'dissolution' of the alliance.

Divergent Co-evolution – This is where the strategic intents of the two firms diverge over time and the rationale behind the strategic alliance is weakening. This weakening may ultimately lead to the dissolution of the alliance.

With regard to the form of the alliance, the parallel type of co-evolution will tend to maintain the form or forms used at establishment, the convergent type will tend to move the alliance towards the 'hierarchical' nature whilst the divergent type will tend to move the alliance towards a 'markets' nature.

An example of this process is the development of the BNP and Dresdner strategic alliance from initiation to dissolution, a process that took place over a 10 year period. It commenced as a response to the commercial opportunities made available by the opening up of Europe to cross-border financial services provision. The alliances' most successful achievements were focussed joint venture operations in the emerging Eastern Europe. As competitors entered those countries with full operations, BNP and Dresdner decided to go it alone and accordingly disbanded the alliance.

The BNP and Dresdner alliance may be characterized, from time zero to time 10 years, as:

- parallel co-evolution – At commencement both banks strategic intents were aligned,
- divergent co-evolution – As country specific concerns, such as the reintegration of East Germany into Germany, impacted on the concerns of top management intents became divergent,

- convergent co-evolution – Simultaneously the position immediately above, the Eastern European joint ventures were a tangible manifestation of convergent intents in relation to those operations,
- divergent co-evolution – As the rationale for the joint ventures, the 'binding agents' of the global alliance declined so the whole alliance diverged to the point of dissolution.

A full exposition of the lifecycle of the BNP/Dresdner alliance is contained in Itschert and ul-Haq (2003).

The three generic cases above are modified by the concept of differential co-evolution. This concept notes that each firm's strategic intent will co-evolve at different rates and that this will have an impact on the nature, purpose, importance, form and validity of the strategic alliance.

The addition of this concept allows three modified categories – differential parallel co-evolution, differential convergent co-evolution, differential divergent co-evolution.

Differential Parallel Co-evolution – This is where the evolution of the strategic intents of the two firms are at different rates but in a broadly similar direction. Whilst this allows the continuation of the alliance, the faster evolving firm, for example, may pull the slower evolving firm and the strategic alliance in a new joint direction.

Differential Convergent Co-evolution – This is where the strategic intents of the two firms evolve at different rates but in a convergent direction. Whilst this allows the continuation of the alliance it may only do so until such time as the faster evolving firm, for example, decides to internalize the alliance and the slower evolving firm, inside its boundaries.

Differential Divergent Co-evolution – This is where the evolution of the strategic intents of the two firms is at different rates but in a divergent direction. The faster evolving firm, for example, if it finds benefits from the strategic alliance may internalize it or on the other hand it may evolve beyond the alliance.

The three generic, and three sub-generic, concepts above point to the complexity of the concept of anticipated durability. The complexity of the real situation is many layered with:

- the speed of evolution of each firm's strategic intent changing over time with spurts of innovation interspersed with moments of complacency,

- changes in the nature of co-evolution over time with parallel, convergent and divergent (and differential) episodes being interspersed,
- exponential increases in complexity if more than two firms are members of the strategic alliance with all the firms, and the strategic alliance, being subject to co-evolution of their respective strategic intents. All six classifications of co-evolution (and many intermediate positions) may subsist at the same time in a multi-member alliance,
- the differential effects of the internal and external forces that tend towards inspiration, innovation, and conversely, complacency and atrophy in firms' strategic intents,
- the further increase in complexity of co-evolution in alliances in few-party and many-party situations.

In an increasingly dynamic and (often discontinuous) change orientated commercial environment, a firm's ability to re-configure its strategic intent rapidly, and to implement this intent, is a core competence as suggested earlier. The strategic alliance is one mechanism to assist in this process. If the alliance provides no collaborative advantage then it will be abandoned or allowed to atrophy.

The co-evolution model presented here is our own idea rather than something taken from the academic literature. We feel it has been helpful here in throwing light on alliance persistence and alliance termination. At the same time, precisely because it is new this model may benefit from critical development by others.

The co-evolution model and real option theory

It is possible that valuable insights into the process of effective co-evolution in both strategic and infrastructure alliances can be obtained by combining the proposed research on the new 'The Co-Evolution Model' with the existing 'Real Option Theory'. A migration of 'option models ... from financial markets to corporate decision making' has been seen (Kogut and Kulatilaka, 2004). In 'strategically interesting settings ... having made an initial investment, firms can actively engage in follow-on activities that can influence outcomes and identify new possible actions and goals.' (Adner and Levinthal, 2004). The Co-Evolution Model by the author allows for the continuous re-configuration of an alliance (or set of alliances) – at all levels from strategic intent to operational delivery – and adds to the current debate. Adner and Levinthal (2004) suggest that real options, should not be used only to 'engage in some prespecified opportunity set' but rather they should be used in a more flexible way, combining 'a real options logic for initiating investments ... [with] ... an organisational design that can abandon initiatives efficiently' thereby allowing rapid and fluid co-evolution. It is beyond the scope of this research to examine this confluence of interest and models, but others may well wish to develop this area.

Appendix 1　Research Methodology

Philosophical underpinnings

Epistemology

All research activity has embedded in it a theory of knowledge, an epistemology. This theory may be implicit or, as below, explicit; it may be acknowledged or tacit. Regardless of its implicit or explicit status, the embedded theory underpins the research activity and influences its validity, methods and scope. At this stage in the book it is appropriate to make explicit the epistemology employed and its impact on the research methods used.

The epistemological continuum

This continuum ranges from positivism to idealism (or phenomenology), with empiricism, realism and subjectivity in between. Each position on the continuum delineates a different view of the nature of the object-subject relationship in research activity. The boundaries between each position on the continuum are not fixed and are permeable. The researcher's position on the continuum determines the understanding of the nature of the interactions between cause and effect. Furthermore it delineates the position of theory in the research activity – that is, whether the starting point is the existing theory or the subject of the research and whether the end point, accordingly, is proof of the theory or the development of new theories.

i)　Positivism
The positivist epistemology holds the view that the nature of the relationships between the world-at-large and individuals can be observed and explained in the manner of the natural sciences. The researcher is considered remote, or detached, from the social world being investigated. The prediction and explanation of the behaviour of phenomena and the pursuit of objectivity become paramount. A direct cause and effect relationship in human behaviour is deemed to exist, and the researcher attempts to identify these covering laws of human behaviour. In research terms this perspective leads to the use of methods that emphasize the clarity, generalizability and repeatability of outcomes. Specifically such research often progresses from theory, through the generation of hypothesizes, to questionnaire based surveys resulting in statistically significant, and therefore generalizable, findings.

Such epistemology and its related research methods generally attempt to reduce the complex, interrelated world into easily measured, and often simplistic, formulations. At its best this view can provide insights into specific aspects of complex issues. At its worst it assumes that the controlled environment of the laboratory, prevalent in the natural sciences and necessary for replicating and therefore generalizing findings, is in principle repeatable in the highly complex social world of individuals, firms and markets.

ii)   Idealism or Phenomenology

This diametrically opposed view holds that social reality is constructed by the many varied interactions between social actors and between the social actors and their non-human environment. The researcher must extract meaning by understanding individual's interpretation of events and actions. Accordingly the researcher needs to interact directly with the phenomena (the social world microcosm) under investigation. Here the researcher attempts to gather rich, contextually specific (and therefore not generalizable) data. From this the researcher theorizes and attempts to build an understanding of the social world as arising from the 'culture', whether national, corporate or group, under study. The resulting, generally qualitative, research method often involves a degree of immersion in the 'culture' under study (ethnographic research for example) on the part of the researcher. Bhaskar (1975) refers to this position as 'transcendental idealism' and notes that 'the objects of scientific knowledge are models' and that 'such objects are artificial constructs and ... they are not independent of men or human activity in general'.

The view of social actors together creating a 'reality' has been largely abandoned and replaced by an acknowledgement of the impact of external realities – for example, national culture, education and 'systems' on our actions and opportunities.

Table A1.1 provides a summary of this continuum.

The positivist view of research is dependent on a 'closed-systems' approach where the aim of the closed system is to control conditions of the experiment so that regularities can be identified in the form of 'whenever event x then event y' (Clark, 2000). The idealist or transcendental idealist approach is based on an open system, or emergent, approach where the mechanisms are considered or 'imagined to produce the phenomena in question' (Bhaskar, 1975).

Between these two extremes lie Empiricism, Subjectivity and, in the centre, Realism.

iii)   Empiricism

At the heart of the Empiricist perspective is the view that data gathered by the researcher about the social world is independent of the interpretation of this data. Accurate data collection requires the use of 'neutral' measuring instruments. The data does not prove or disprove a theory (à la Positivism) but leads to the researcher considering the data as the end result. The data makes its own statements and these are the outcomes of the research. Bhaskar terms this 'classical empiricism' and notes that 'science is conceived as a kind of automatic or behavioural response to the stimulus of given facts or their conjunctions' (Bhaskar, 1975).

iv)   Subjectivity

In this perspective what matters is the 'meanings that people give to their environment, not the environment itself'. The social environment which the individual inhabits is dependent on the individual's understanding and interpretation of it.

v)   The Realist Perspective

The Realist perspective is in the centre of his continuum. Rejecting the claims of positivism this perspective has at its core the view that 'all analytical work in the

Table A1.1 The Epistemological Continuum (1) and the Logic of Scientific Discovery (2)

Characteristics	Empiricism	Realism	Subjectivity	Characteristics
Research is remote from the social world under investigation				Researcher has direct experiential contact with the phenomena under investigation
Cause and effect relationship deemed to exist and attempts made to identify				Reality is socially constructed by the myriad interactions between social actors
Generalizable, repeatable and clear outcomes attainable				Researcher gathers rich, contextually specific data and then theorizes
(1) Positivism	Empiricism	Realism	Subjectivity	Idealism/Phenomenology
(2)	Classical Empiricism	Transcendental Realism		Transcendental Idealism

Sources: (2) Bhaskar (1975)

social sciences cannot be undertaken within the closed system model' (Clark, 2000). It further holds that the mechanisms, or ways of working or acting, are not imaginary (unproved), as stated in transcendental idealism, but rather 'may be real, or come to be established as such' (Bhaskar, 1975). Realism has at its foundation the attempt to uncover the structures of social relations in order to understand why we have the policies and practices we do. Furthermore, realist research requires the investigation of the underlying mechanisms that make those [social interactions] possible in the first instance. Thus 'reality' is not the individuals' perception and interpretation of the 'world' they live in, with each individual's reality being unique and unrepeatable (and presumably unshareable). 'Society' is not just a conglomeration of a number of individual perceptions. Rather through continued, iterative, empirical testing (using a number of mutually *inclusive* quantitative and qualitative research methods), this real world may also come to be known as 'real'. This empirical testing leads us to determine the 'generative mechanisms in models' Bhaskar (1975) the observed events that lead to the construction of a model. In Figure A1.1 this is shown as the movement from position (2) where the researcher imagines that the world in constructed in the particular way, through empirical testing to a point (3) where the researcher has greater confidence in asserting that this is how the world is which allows the researcher to build a model (M) of that world.

vi) Transcendental Realism

Transcendental realism attempts to link our perception of the world-at-large (the imagined world) with reality (the real world) through the empirical testing process. Transcendental realism regards the objects of knowledge to be the 'structures and mechanisms that generate phenomena; and the knowledge as produced in the social activity of science' (Bhaskar, 1975).

According to this position, the world is made up of three domains: the 'empirical', consisting of experience, impression, perception; the 'actual', consisting of events and state of affairs; and the 'deep' consisting of the underlying structures, powers, mechanisms and tendencies.

Lawson (1997) states that these often undetected 'deep' domain structures, powers, mechanisms and tendencies (as defined in Table A1.2 and Table A1.3) underpin and facilitate real events and that these different domains of reality (1, 2 and 3 in Figure A1.1) are out of '[time] phase' with each other.

Thus the transcendental realist epistemology leads to the nature of scientific inquiry being aimed 'at identifying and illuminating the structures and mechanisms, powers and tendencies that govern and facilitate the course of events' (Lawson, 1997) through a process of *retroduction*. Retroduction 'consists in the movement ... from the conception of some phenomenon of interest to a conception of some totally different type of thing, mechanism, structure or condition that, at least in part, is responsible for the given phenomenon' (Lawson, 1997). The process of retroduction thereby moves the inquirer from the 'empirical' and 'actual' domains into the 'deep' domain.

From transcendental realism to research

The forgoing has introduced the concepts of Realism (Bhaskar, 1975) and Transcendental Realism (Lawson, 1997). This section considers the application of the latter to the research conducted and reported in this book.

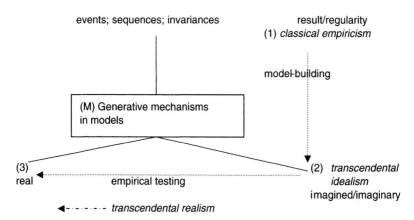

Figure A1.1 The Logic of Scientific Discovery, adapted from Diagram 3.1
Source: Bhaskar (1975)

Table A1.2 Transcendental Realism versus Empirical Realism

Objects

Domain	Transcendental Realism	Empirical Realism
'deep'	structures powers mechanisms tendencies	
'actual'	events state of affairs	Events state of affairs
'empirical'	experience impression perception	Experience impression perception

Source: Adapted from Lawson (1997)

One example of the application of this approach to the broad area of this book is to consider the issue of capital in banking. The observed 'actual' domain 'state of affairs' is that the banking industry is said to have the greatest volume of capital allocated to any industry worldwide. The retroductive approach would be to try to identify the 'deep' domain reasons why this observed phenomenon obtains. Thus one brief possible analysis might be in terms of the following structures, powers, mechanisms and tendencies.

Structures – that Government policy generally restricts to authorized institutions the provision of loans to households and firms; the Bank for International

Table A1.3 Definitions of Transcendental Realism Deep Domain Categories

Category	Definition
Structures	Systems and complexly structured situations
Powers	Potentials, capacities, abilities to act in certain ways; facilitate various activities and developments
Mechanisms	A way of acting or working of a structured thing; a causal power of things
Tendencies	Continuing activity; potentialities which may be exercised or in play without being directly realized or manifest in any particular outcome; a power that is being exercised whatever events ensue

Source: After Lawson (1997)

Settlements (BIS) demands that banks hold a minimum level of capital; many intra-country financial systems are connected to the non-bank international capital markets.

Powers – that financial institutions have the power to redistribute funds by acting as intermediaries, for example, from individuals to firms, from depositors to borrowers and to lengthen the period of loans over the period of deposits.

Mechanisms – that banks facilitate entrepreneurship and commercial activity by increasing the flow of credit.

Tendencies – that bankers are less risk averse than governments.

A more generic approach is suggested by Sayer (1992) wherein he focuses on the movement from concrete observed events to abstract underlying mechanisms and tendencies.

This general approach of attempting to determine the 'deep' domain causes of observed events is used to analyze the industry and firm level trends of European banking sector strategic alliances. The following section details the research methodologies used.

Research design

This research consists of three empirical elements: desk research, a questionnaire based postal survey and thematic semi-structured interviews. The approach leads to multifaceted findings based on published annual reviews of trends (Chapter Two), directed and closed questionnaire responses (Chapter Four) and an open-ended discussion process (Chapter Five). The research design encapsulates these three elements so as to add greater depth and validity to the findings compared to what would be possible using only one empirical method. Furthermore the source data is broad based enough to attempt to tease out the structures, powers, mechanisms and tendencies underpinning the use of strategic alliances in the European banking sector.

The desk research was carried out to determine the historical propensity of banks to cooperate, to identify the 23 year trend towards increased liberalization in financial markets and to determine the lifecycles of strategic alliances in the 1970s, 1980s and early 1990s. This was reported in Chapter Two. An extensive review of the strategy field and the literature on strategic alliances was reported in Chapter Three. This was used to identify the nature of the subject under investigation, the strategic alliance. The questionnaire research was carried out and was reported in Chapter Four. The analysis of the interview transcripts based on the themes identified in Chapter One and Three was then conducted and written up.

This book reports a number of research activities carried out in one industry over a period of time. It provides a high level review of the major trends supported by a range of research findings.

Part 1: desk research

The desk research was carried out to set the context of this book in relation to 'actual' events occurring in the research area. The primary purpose was to identify the pre-existing (in general) and current (in Europe) propensity of banks to enter into a number of types of alliances. Three public sources of trends in the banking sector were obtained and analyzed: *The Financial Times World Banking* special section (published annually*), The Economist Survey of International Banking* (published annually) and The Bank of England *Quarterly Bulletin* section on *Developments in International Banking and Capital Markets*. These were obtained for the 23-year period ending in December 1993. This period was chosen to stretch far enough into the past so as to allow in-depth analysis of the Clubs and Consortium Banks lifecycle, (and the underlying changes in the economic, political and business environment), strategy and a limited analysis of the Bankassurance and Virtual-Bank lifecycles.

The analysis was carried out by identifying the concrete events mentioned in the data sources, as detailed in Chapter Two, and attempting to identify the mechanisms and structures that underpinned those events. The data sources used were public analyses of the major occurrences in the banking sector. An event mentioned here could be deemed to be of major importance on the basis that a quarterly or annual review in such reputable publications, would only report the major and important events.

In undertaking research the generally preferred method is to undertake primary research through a variety of data gathering methods. In this part of the research, however, secondary sources have been exclusively used. The data ranges over a vast 23-year period, and it was therefore impossible to access primary sources for analysis within the time and resource constraints of this book. This section constitutes one third of the empirical part of the research – the remaining questionnaire and interviews are primary data. The data sources used are considered to be reputable chroniclers of primary events. The first two would have reported the primary events in real time (daily and weekly respectively) and would have used these reports as the basis for identifying the core events in preparing the annual review. The third source reported events on a quarterly basis. It is, therefore, possible to assert that these provide a valid reflection of the real events that occurred and their relatively high importance.

Part 2: Questionnaire based postal survey

The questionnaire based postal survey was conducted over 20 countries in the continent of Europe. The purpose was to provide an empirical foundation, based on primary research, for understanding the prevalent practices and motivations (entering, forming, managing and evolving strategic alliances) in the major banks in this region. Furthermore the survey tested the definition of a strategic alliance proposed, and elicited agreement to and served as a foundation for a follow up interview.

The sample selection and survey process was split into two by the geographical location of the centre of strategic decision-making (normally the location of the head office and board of directors).

With regard to the United Kingdom, the initial sample list included all banks registered in the UK and considered by the Bank of England to be of 'British' origin. These banks were also considered to be managed in a strategic sense in the UK. The list consisted of 63 banks.

One bank was later excluded from this list, at their request, as all strategic decisions were made by the parent bank located overseas. A UK merchant bank owned by an overseas bank retained its place in the list, as the strategic decisions for the UK firm were taken in the UK. Three banks were reclassified as overseas continental European and therefore part of the continental European sample. This reduced the UK sample to 59.

A personally addressed letter was sent detailing the research agenda and enclosing a questionnaire and a university pen. The wording of the personally addressed initial letter is given in Table A1.4.

In drafting the initial letter, four considerations were of particular importance: to assure confidentiality, to gain an agreement in principle to a follow-up interview, to enhance the response rates and to test the strategic alliance definition used. The confidentiality and interview issues were mentioned both in the text of the questionnaire and in the covering letter.

Attempts were made to enhance the response rate by printing the letter on the university letterhead. The letter was signed by a professor and the author to try to ensure equivalence in seniority between the first signatory on the letter and the named recipient. A university pen was enclosed as a free gift to facilitate the completion of the questionnaire and to raise the response rate and as a 'thank you' to the respondent. A pre-paid response envelope was also provided to reduce barriers to returning the questionnaire.

The alliance definition used in this book, based on the work detailed in Chapter Two, was enclosed in the letter. The author noted that a substantial variety of definitions are used in the academic literature and by practitioners. Including a definition in the questionnaire would go some way towards putting respondents on the same footing. Half a page was made available for respondents to disagree with the given definition or propose an alternative.

With regard to Continental Europe, *The Banker* magazine, a trade journal, publishes an annual list of banks ranked by total asset size. The 'Top 500 Europeans' listing was reviewed, and all banks which had a total asset size of over US\$10 000 million were included in the list. This asset size was chosen to include the major continental European banks (which should include at least one bank in each of 19 continental European countries as detailed in Table A1.4) and exclude those of the approximately 3000 banks in continental Europe whose operations are, in comparison, mainly regional and small scale.

Table A1.4   Text of Initial Letter Sent with Questionnaire

<u>Strategic Alliances in Banking Survey</u>

The university recently received funding for a study of the role of strategic alliances within the banking sector. As part of this study, we are anxious to survey the views of banks themselves towards this particular form of commercial development.

We are writing to request your assistance in this research and would be most grateful if you, or an appropriate senior colleague, could complete the attached short questionnaire and return it to us in the reply-paid envelope.

There is no precise or agreed definition of a strategic alliance. For the purposes of this exercise our preferred definition is 'A durable relationship established between two or more independent firms involving the sharing or pooling of resources to create a mechanism (corporate or otherwise) for undertaking a business activity or activities of strategic importance to one or more partners for their mutual economic advantage'.

We would therefore ask you, in responding to our questionnaire, to consider any relationship you have formed which appears to meet these criteria:

- The relationship should be seen as a lasting, not temporary, one.
- The partners involved should be independent of one another (i.e., one should not be a subsidiary of the other, though minority shareholdings are acceptable).
- Purely operational relationships (e.g., Correspondent banking links) should be excluded: the relationship must be seen to be of strategic importance to at least one of the partners.
- The alliance need not involve the creation of a fully-owned subsidiary, but there must be some sharing or pooling of resources to qualify – if only resources of proprietary knowledge or customer information.
- Thus normal buyer-supplier relationships would be excluded, but long-term vertical links, involving (say) the outsourcing of a key activity would be included.

A space is provided in the questionnaire for your additional thoughts regarding the nature of strategic alliances in banking.

Any information that you provide will be treated with complete confidentiality. No analysis in our resulting research output will mention you or your organization.

We will be happy to provide you with a copy of the report if you indicate your interest on the questionnaire and would appreciate the opportunity to conduct a short follow-up interview at your convenience.

The primary objective of this research is the enhancement of applied and academic research in banking and alliances and its dissemination to the academic and financial services communities throughout the world. Your assistance in this can help us to achieve this objective.

If you require any further information, please do not hesitate to contact us.

Source: Definition from ul-Haq *et al* (1996)

As with the United Kingdom sample, contact details were obtained from the *Bankers Almanac*. In the majority of cases the name of the managing director was given. In cases of uncertainty, a telephone call was made to the personal assistant of the managing director to obtain the correct contact details. A covering letter, questionnaire and university pen were sent to each bank and a follow up reminder letter sent to 117 banks.

A total of 17 completed questionnaires were returned by the UK sample. A follow up telephone call was made to 15 banks to arrange an interview and seven interviews were held. A total of 51 completed questionnaires were returned by the Continental European sample. A follow up telephone call was made to 20 banks to arrange an interview and 17 interviews were held. The sample and responses breakdown is given in Table A1.5.

The returned questionnaires were first graded into three groups:

- valid responses where the respondent had attempted to complete the questionnaire;
- specific non-questionnaire responses, where the respondent did not complete the questionnaire but volunteered information in some other form;
- no valid response items, where the recipient wrote to decline the completing of the questionnaire.

Valid responses totalled 68 completed questionnaires. These were coded and input into the SPSS for Windows statistical software and a set of frequencies computed for the 44 questions asked in the survey. These responses are analyzed and reported in Chapter Four of this book.

The survey attempts to provide a broad view of the practice of large banking firms with regard to their strategic alliances. It encompasses 20 countries across Europe (UK, Western and some Eastern Europe) while surveying the largest 217 banks in this geographical area.

This broad approach is appropriate in the context of a book that is focussed on large firms and cross-border alliances. However, this limits the nature and degree of statistical analysis that can be carried out. With a valid response size of 68 and numbers of valid responses per country ranging from nil to 16 with an average of 4.5, it is not possible to carry out a statistically significant analysis even when using the Nonparametric Test version of the Chi-Square Test. The appropriate method is to use the frequencies output as mentioned above.

The survey therefore provides a broad view of practice. While outside the gambit of this book, there is scope for a survey of all banks located in the geographical area, unrestricted as to size, thereby generating a sample of over 3000 possible respondents. This approach would lend itself to more detailed statistical analysis.

Part 3: Thematic, semi-structured interviews

Interviews were conducted with 24 senior managers across nine European countries and were designed to provide insights into the manager's perceptions of the issues facing their firms in the alliance process.

The initial questionnaire sent out in the postal survey, as detailed above, included a space at the end for administrative questions. Question 12 asked if

Table A1.5   Analysis of Study Sample, Valid Questionnaire Responses and
Interviews Held

Area/Country	Total Sample	Valid Responses as % of Sample	Number of Interviews
Total: UK	59	29	7
Total: C-Europe	158	32	17
Total: UK+CE	217	31	24
CE Countries			
Austria	7	14	
Belgium	8	50	2
Bulgaria	1		
Chez. Republic	1		
Denmark	5	20	
Finland	4		
France	17	18	2
Germany	43	37	5
Greece	2	50	
Ireland	3	100	
Italy	24	17	
Luxembourg	4	25	
Holland	6	83	2
Norway	3	67	2
Portugal	5	20	
Spain	10	20	1
Sweden	5	60	1
Switzerland	9	44	2
Turkey	1		

the respondent 'Would be willing, in principle, to participate in a follow-up interview?' with a yes/no possible answer. Question 13 asked for the contact details of the respondent. Respondents who ticked the 'yes' box in question 12 were contacted with a view to re-confirm their willingness to be interviewed, and interviews were arranged as appropriate. A letter detailing the research agenda, the format and broad questions to be raised in the interview and confirming the logistical details was sent to the interviewee. Thus the sample was semi-self-selecting and well briefed prior to the interview being conducted.

A total of 24 interviews in nine European countries were conducted. The interview travel, accommodation and transcription costs were funded by, variously, the Banking Centre and the International Research Group – both at Loughborough University Business School, the Birmingham Business School at the University of Birmingham, and the British Council offices in Basel, Madrid and Paris. Interviews were conducted in English at the head office of the subject bank. In the main they were tape-recorded always with the explicit knowledge and consent of the interviewee and lasted on average 45 minutes to 1 hour, though some took as long as 1 1/2 hours. In some cases another academic accompanied the author.

The interviews were semi-structured in nature, asking the following questions:

i)   What are the key environmental or competitive issues that your bank faces?
ii) What alliances has the bank entered into and why?
iii) How does the bank go about forming an alliance?
iv) How do you manage an alliance relationship?
v)   How do you allow and encourage an alliance to evolve?

The semi-structured nature of the interview allowed the interviewer to interact with the interviewee and to gain access to the interviewee's 'accounts and articulations' and to allow them to 'be recounted' (Mason, 1996).

A 'grounded theory' approach was taken in the interview process. Thus the purpose was, from an initial set of broad research questions, to generate, collect and analyze data from which theory could be built (Punch, 1998).

The locus of strategic decision-making in large organizations is generally considered to be at head office level, though some debate between the emergent and traditional schools of thought does exist. Even if the decision process is an emergent one the final responsibility to articulate the strategic goals, vision, of the bank lies at or near the Board. Interviewees in this sample were mainly main board members (15 out of 24) or a head office executive (nine out of 24). The interviewees were drawn from the strategic decision-makers and they ranged from members of German and Swiss banks' supervisory boards, chief executives and executive directors to corporate planning managers and similar head office officials. The sample was broadly representative of a wide geographical scope, with the subject banks being classified into four categories: regional (for example, German Landesbanken), national, international (mainstream national banks with a significant international presence) and global (banks with a substantial presence in most continents). The head offices of the banks at which interviews were conducted were located in the nine European countries visited. In ownership terms a distinction was drawn between joint stock and cooperative banks. The former are those owned by shareholders, whether public or private sector, while the latter include cooperative and mutual banks (that is, those 'owned' by their members or customers). This analysis is summarized in the matrices in Tables A1.6 and Table A1.7.

Table A1.6   Analysis of Country of Interview and the Responsibility Level of Interviewee

Country/ Responsibility level	Supervisory Board	Chairman	Main Board	Head Office Executive	Subsidiary Board	Total
Belgium				2		2
France		2				2
Germany			2	3		5
Holland			1	1		2
Norway			2			2
Spain			1			1
Sweden			1			1
Switzerland	2					2
United Kingdom			4	3		7
Total	2	2	11	9		24

The responses to the interviews were first disaggregated into the process of the alliance – from formation to dissolution – and an analysis written (provided in Chapter Five) that sought to identify and distil the major concerns of the managers interviewed.

At the start of each interview the interviewee was assured that all comments and observations made would be treated in the strictest confidence and was asked whether the interview could be taped. Only those who consented were tape recorded.

It did not appear that the interviewees were being more guarded when the tape-recorder was being used. The responses seemed to be genuine and comprehensive. After each interview, recorded or otherwise, a file note was made of the main issues discussed. Each taped interview was transcribed verbatim. These accounts, along with any file notes and interview notes, were used as the source documents in the analysis. Thus the data gathered was rich and contextually specific and consisted of the 'knowledge, views, understandings, interpretations, experiences' (Mason, 1996) of the interviewees coupled with the author's analysis.

Only nine of the interviews were held in the UK. In the UK interviews one was conducted with a German national working for a British bank. The

Table A1.7   Analysis of Country of Interview and Geographical
Operational Scope of Joint Stock and Cooperative Banks

Country/ Geographical Scope	Mainly Regional	Mainly National	International	Global	Total ( )	Ttoal [ ]	Grand Total
Belgium		(1) [1]			1	1	2
France		(1)	(1)		2		2
Germany	[1]	(1) [2]		(1)	2	3	5
Holland				[2]		2	2
Norway		(1)		(1)	2		2
Spain		(1)			1		1
Sweden		(1)			1		1
Switzerland	(1)		(1)		2		2
United Kingdom	(1)	(2) [1]	(1)	(2)	6	1	7
Total ( )	2	8	3	4	17		
Total [ ]	1	4		2		7	
Grand total	3	12	3	6			24

Key: ( ) = Joint Stock Banks
      [ ] = Cooperative Banks

remaining interviews were conducted with nationals, as far as one could tell, of the country of origin of the bank. In the case of interviews held in continental Europe, although the English language was ostensibly a second language, this was not considered problematic as the international language of business and banking is English and because all interviewees displayed fluent English language skills.

The primary issue in any interview process, especially one that is not strongly structured, is to develop a meaningful dialogue between interviewer and interviewee (a subjective relationship) while eliciting the more objective insights of the interviewee. Many methodologists have commented on the need for this continuous balancing act.

To achieve the successful completion of interviews there are three necessary conditions that need to be met: accessibility, cognition and motivation.

The term 'accessibility' relates to a decision about whether the interviewee has the knowledge that the interviewer seeks. In these interviews the interviewees were semi-self-selecting in response to a questionnaire about strategic alliances.

Furthermore all the interviewees were located at the top end of their firm's hierarchy, a place generally considered to be the locus of strategic decision-making.

The term 'cognition' relates to the interviewees understanding their role and what is expected of them in the interview. Prior to each interview the basic parameters were made explicit in a letter confirming the interview and then again verbally at the start of the interview. These parameters were: type (semi-structured), context (rich contextual addition to questionnaires), topic (strategic alliances) and time constraints (amount of interviewee's time requested).

The term 'motivation' refers to the need for interviewees to be aware that their thoughts and ideas on the interview subject were of value to the interviewer and the research. This value was displayed through respondents being asked in the questionnaire if they would be willing to be interviewed thereby indicating that the interviews were an integral part of the study. Their semi-self-selection also shows that interviewees considered that they had some further insights that would add value to the research. Finally, through the encouraging nature of the probing or follow up questions and the obvious interest in the interviewee's observations shown by the interviewer, value was shown to the respondents.

All three criteria of accessibility, cognition and motivation were met in the establishment and conduct of the interviews. The interviews can therefore be broadly termed successful in gathering valuable data.

Reflections on methodology

The methodologies employed in this research are detailed above. To reflect on their appropriateness and on the way it all worked out in practice may be helpful.

Questionnaire

The original research agenda was to consider substantial cross-border alliances and accordingly the sample of banks in 20 countries, on the continent of Europe, broadly defined, was subject to a qualifying hurdle, namely an asset size of over US$10 000 billion. The resulting small response did not generate findings that may have been of general importance, rather provided insights for further investigation. Not using the asset size hurdle would have led to a potential sample size of approximately 3000 banks and allowed more statistical validation of findings and captured data on a wider range of in-country alliances.

The questions were formed using a five point Likert scale ranging from 'strongly agree' to 'strongly disagree' and a broad bi-polarity established in reporting the findings. On reflection, if a ranking and rating system had been used in the design of the questionnaire then a finer degree of discrimination in the views of respondents could have been identified and reported.

Literature

The very substantial, and international, underpinning literature regarding alliances was filtered through the medium of the editors of major international journals and collections. This process resulted in over 400 papers being analyzed. An alternative, and equally acceptable, method would have been to use the Citation Index to gauge the influence of a particular academic paper on thought in the alliances field and to build an analysis from these papers.

Control group

Our study raises the question of the existential status of the control group. The questionnaire was completed by banks who were both willing and relatively qualified in the sense of having experience of strategic alliances. The control group is all those banks who excluded themselves on the grounds that they had no relevant activity on which they could report. And the interview sample was determined by the questionnaire sample, where questionnaire respondents were asked to indicate whether they were willing to be interviewed as well, on the grounds of having 'something to say'. In short this research operation casts some doubt on the standard view that the researcher either has a control group or has not, by opening up the possibility of the self-selection of research groups and the implicit control group.

Triangulation

Our research did not use this technique of triangulation as formally defined. On the other hand it did use a variety of methodological thrusts – desk research, literature analysis, interviews and a survey – and we would like to suggest that this multiple methodology has enriched the findings. In particular it has enabled our leverage of the definition of the strategic alliance and has facilitated our reconstruction of the theory of the firm.

Conclusion

The research has been designed to examine the research question 'Do Strategic Alliances Add Value?' at industry and firm level in Europe. Through analysis of the foundation theory (Coase, 1937), a historical review, a questionnaire survey and in-depth interviews the book attempts to provide a multi-dimensional examination of the research question.

References

Abrahamson, E (1996) Management Fashion. *Academy of Management Review*, **21**(1), 254–85.

Adner, R and Levinthal, D A (2004) Real Options and Real Tradeoffs. *Academy of Management Review*, **29**(1), 120–6.

Afriyie, K (1988) A Technology-Transfer Methodology for Developing Joint Production Strategies in Varying Technological Systems. In: *Cooperative Strategies in International Business*, 81–95. Eds. Contractor, F J and Lorange P. New York: Lexington Books.

Afuah, A (2000) How Much do your Co-opetitors' Capabilities Matter in the Face of Technological Change? *Strategic Management Journal*, (Special Issue) **21**(3), 387–404.

Ahuja, G (2000) The Duality of Collaboration: Inducements and Opportunities in the Formation of Interfirm Linkages. *Strategic Management Journal*, (Special Issue) **21**(3), 317–43.

Aldrich, H E (1979) *Organisations Evolving*. London: Sage.

Anand, B N and Khanna, T (2000) Do Firms Learn to Create Value: The Case of Alliances. *Strategic Management Journal*, (Special Issue) **21**(3), 295–315.

Anand, J, Ainuddin, R A and Makino, S (1997) An Empirical Analysis of Multi-national Strategy and International Joint Venture Characteristics in Japanese MNCs. In: *Cooperative Strategies: Asian Pacific Perspectives*, 325–40. Eds. Beamish, P W and Killing, J P. San Francisco: The New Lexington Press.

Ansoff, H I (1965) Corporate Strategy. Homewood, Illinois: Dow Jones-Irwin.

Argyris, C and Schon, D (1978) *Organisational Learning: A Theory of Action Perspective*. Reading, Mass: Addison-Wesley.

Ari'o, A (1997) Veracity and Commitments: Cooperative Behaviour in First-Time Collaborative Ventures. In: *Cooperative Strategies: Asian Pacific Perspectives*, 215–41. Eds. Beamish, P W and Killing, J P. San Francisco: The New Lexington Press.

Ari'o, A and Torre, J de la (1998) Learning from Failure: Towards an Evolutionary Model of Collaborative Ventures. *Organization Science*, **9**(3), 306–25.

Asvathitanont, C (1997) *Strategic Alliance: Key Factor of Success In Planning and Implementing*. Unpublished Master of Business Administration dissertation, University of Birmingham.

Aulakh, P S, Kotabe, M and Sahay, A (1997) Trust and Performance in Cross-Border Marketing Partnerships: A Behavioural Approach. In: *Cooperative Strategies: North American Perspectives*, 163–96. Eds. Beamish, P W and Killing, J P. San Francisco: The New Lexington Press.

Axelrod, R (1984) *The Evolution of Cooperation*. New York: HarperCollins.

Bank of England Quarterly Bulletin (1973) Speech by the Governor of the Bank of England. **13**(1), 56–9.

Bank of England Quarterly Bulletin (1975) Statistical annex, Table 8/10 Other overseas banks & 8/11 Other UK banks. **15**(1).

Bank of England Quarterly Bulletin (1976) Statistical annex, Table 2/10 Consortium banks. **16**(1).

Barkema, H G, Shenkar, O, Vermeulen, F and Bell, J H (1997) Working Abroad, Working with Others: How Firms Learn to Operate International Joint Ventures. *The Academy of Management Journal*, **40**(2), 426–42.

Barnes, J W, Crook, M H, Koybaeva, Taira and Stafford, E R (1997) Why Our Russian Alliances Fail. *Long Range Planning*, **20**(4), 540–50.

Barney, J B (1991) Firm resources and sustained competitive advantage. *Journal of Management*, **17**, 99–120.

Baum, J A C, Calabrese, T and Silverman, B S (2000) Don't Go It Alone: Alliance Network Composition and Startups' Performance in Canadian Biotechnology. *Strategic Management Journal*, (Special Issue) **21**(3), 267–94.

Beamish, P W, Killing, J P (1997) Cooperative Strategies: Asia Pacific (North American, European) Perspectives, San Francisco: The New Lexington Press.

Beamish, P W and Delios, A (1997a) Incidence and Propensity of Alliance Formation. In: *Cooperative Strategies: Asian Pacific Perspectives*, 91–114. Eds. Beamish, P W and Killing, J P. San Francisco: The New Lexington Press.

Beamish, P W and Delios, A (1997b) Improving Joint Venture Performance Through Congruent Measures of Success. In: *Cooperative Strategies: Asian Pacific Perspectives*, 103–27. Eds. Beamish, P W and Killing, J P. San Francisco: The New Lexington Press.

Bell, J H J, Barkema, H G and Verbeke, A (1997) An Eclectic Model of the Choice Between Wholly Owned Subsidiaries and Joint Ventures as Modes of Foreign Entry. In: *Cooperative Strategies: Asian Pacific Perspectives*, 128–57. Eds. Beamish, P W and Killing, J P. San Francisco: The New Lexington Press.

Berg, S V and Hoekman J M (1988) Entrepreneurship over the Product Life Cycle: Joint Venture Strategies in the Netherlands. In: *Cooperative Strategies in International Business*, 145–67. Eds. Contractor, F J and Lorange, P. New York: Lexington Books.

Bettis, R A and Hitt, M A (1995) The New Competitive Landscape, *Strategic Management Journal*, **16**, 7–19.

Bhaskar, R (1975) *A Realist Theory of Science*. Versdo.

Boddy, D, Macbeth, D and Wagner, B (1988) Implementing Co-operative Strategy: An empirically-based Model of Supply Chain Partnering. *Fifth International Conference on Multi-Organisational Partnerships & Co-operative Strategy*. Conference paper, July. Balliol, Oxford.

Borys, B and Jemison, D B (1993) Hybrid Arrangements in Strategic Alliances: Theoretical Issues in Organizational Combinations. In: *Multinational Strategic Alliances*, 33–58. Ed: Culpan, R. New York: International Business Press.

Bouchikhi, H, Rond, M de and Leroux, V (1998) Process and Evolution in Alliances. *Fifth International Conference on Multi-Organisational Partnerships & Co-operative Strategy*. Conference paper, July. Balliol, Oxford.

Bourgeois, L J (1984) Strategic Management and Determinism. *Academy of Management Review*, **9**(4), 568–96.

Buckley, P J and Casson, M (1988) A Theory of Cooperation in International Business. In: *Cooperative Strategies in International Business*, 31–53. Eds. Contractor, F J and Lorange, P. New York: Lexington Books.

Buckley, P J and Casson, M (1997) An Economic Model of International Joint Venture Strategy. In: *Cooperative Strategies: European Perspectives*, 3–32. Eds. Beamish, P W and Killing, J P. San Francisco: The New Lexington Press.

Burton, J (1995a) Composite Strategy: The Combination of Collaboration and Competition. *Journal of General Management*, **21**(1), 1–23.

Burton, J (1995b) Partnering with the Japanese: Threat or Opportunity for European Businesses? *European Management Journal*, **15**(3), 304–15.

Casti, J (1992) *Images of Man in the Mirror of Science*. London: Scribners.

Chandler, A R (1962) Strategy and Structure: Chapters in the History of the Industrial Enterprise. Cambridge, Mass: MIT Press.

Chi, T (2000) Option to Acquire or Divest a Joint Venture. *Strategic Management Journal*, **21**(6), 665–87.

Child, J and Faulkner, D (1998) *Strategies of Co-operation: Managing Alliances, Networks, and Joint Ventures*. Oxford: Oxford University Press.

Child, J, Yan, Y and Lu, Y (1997) Ownership and Control in Sino-Foreign Joint Ventures. In: *Cooperative Strategies: Asian Pacific Perspectives*, 181–225. Eds. Beamish, P W and Killing, J P. San Francisco: The New Lexington Press.

Choi, C J and Lee, S H (1997) A Knowledge-Based View of Cooperative Inter-organizational Relationships. In: *Cooperative Strategies: European Perspectives*, 33–58. Eds. Beamish, P W and Killing, J P. San Francisco: The New Lexington Press.

Chung, S, Singh, H and Lee, S H (2000) Complementarity, Status Similarity and Social Capital as Drivers of Alliance Formation. *Strategic Management Journal*, **21**(1), 1–23.

Clark, P (2000) *Organizations in Action: Competition Between Contexts*. London: Routledge.

Coase, R H (1937) The Nature of the Firm. *Economics*, **4**, 386–405.

Collins (1995) *Compact English Dictionary*. England: HarperCollins.

Combs, J G and Ketchen Jr, D J (1999) Explaining Interfirm Cooperation and Performance: Toward a Reconciliation of Predictions. *Strategic Management Journal*, **20**(9), 867–88.

Contractor, F J and Lorange, P (1988) Why Should Firms Cooperate? The Strategy and Economics Basis for Cooperative Ventures. In: *Cooperative Strategies in International Business*, 3–30. Eds. Contractor, F J and Lorange P. New York: Lexington Books.

Creed, W E D and Miles, R E (1996) Trust in Organisations: A Conceptual Framework Linking Organisational Forms, Managerial Philosophies, and the Opportunity Cost of Controls. In: *Trust in Organisations: Frontiers of Theory and Research*, 16–38. Ed: Tyler, R M. Thousand Oaks, California: Sage.

Das, T K and Teng, B-S (1999) Managing Risks in Strategic Alliances. *The Academy of Management Executive*, **13**(4), 50–62.

D'Aveni, R (1994) Hypercompetition. New York: Free Press.

De Geus, A P (1988) Planning as Learning. *Harvard Business Review*, **66**(2), 70–4.

Demers, C, Hafsi T, Jørgensen and Molz, R (1997) Industry Dynamics of Cooperative Strategy: Dominant and Peripheral Games. In: *Cooperative Strategies: North American Perspectives*, 111–32. Eds. Beamish, P W and Killing, J P. San Francisco: The New Lexington Press.

Dixon, P H and Weaver, K M (1997) Environmental Determinants and Individual-Level Moderators of Alliance Use. *The Academy of Management Journal*, **40**(2), 404–26.

Dollinger, M J, Golden, P A and Saxton, T (1997) The Effect of Reputation on the Decision to Joint Venture. *Strategic Management Journal*, **18**(2), 127–40.

Doz, Y L (1988) Technology Partnerships Between Larger and Smaller Firms: Some Critical Issues. In: *Cooperative Strategies in International Business*, 317–38. Eds. Contractor, F J and Lorange, P. New York: Lexington Books.

Doz, Y (1998) Keeping Score in Alliances: Process Continuity and Discontinuity. *Fifth International Conference on Multi-Organisational Partnerships & Co-operative Strategy*. Conference paper, July. Balliol, Oxford.

Doz, Y and Prahalad, C K (1993) Managing DNMCs: A Search for a New Paradigm. In: *Organization Theory and the Multinational Corporation*, 24–50. Eds. Ghoshal, S and Westney, D E. London: Macmillan.

Doz, Y L, Olk, P M and Ring, P S (2000) Formation Processes of R&D Consortia: Which Path to Take? Where Does it Lead? *Strategic Management Journal*, (Special Issue) 21(3), 239–66.

Dussauge, P and Garrette, B (1999) *Cooperative Strategy: Competing Successfully Through Strategic Alliances*. Chichester: John Wiley.

Dussauge, P, Garrette, B and Mitchell, A (2000) Learning from Competing Partners: Outcomes and Durations of Scale and Link Alliances in Europe. *Strategic Management Journal*, 21(2), 99–126.

Dyer, J H (1997) Effective Interfirm Collaboration: How Firms Minimize Transaction Costs and Maximize Transaction Value. *Strategic Management Journal*, 18(7), 535–56.

Dyer, J H (1998a) Effective Interfirm Collaboration: How Transactors Simultaneously Achieve High Asset Specificity *and* Low Transaction Costs. *Fifth International Conference on Multi-Organisational Partnerships & Co-operative Strategy*. Conference paper, July. Balliol, Oxford.

Dyer, J H (1998b) Improving Performance by Transforming Arms-Length Relationships to Supplier Partnerships: The Chrysler Case. *Fifth International Conference on Multi-Organisational Partnerships & Co-operative Strategy*. Conference paper, July. Balliol, Oxford.

Dyer, J H and Nobeoka, K (2000) Creating and Managing a High-Performance Knowledge-Sharing Network: The Toyota Case. *Strategic Management Journal*, (Special Issue) 21(3), 345–67.

Dyer, J H and Singh, H (1998) The Relational View: Cooperative Strategy and Sources of Interorganizational Competitive Advantage. *The Academy of Management Review*, 23(4), 660–79.

Dymsza, W A (1988) Successes and Failures of Joint Ventures in Developing Countries: Lessons from Experience. In: *Cooperative Strategies in International Business*, 403–24. Eds. Contractor, F J and Lorange, P. New York: Lexington Books.

Economist, The (1970) International Banking Survey, 14 November.

Economist, The (1973) The Survey of International Banking, 27 January.

Economist, The (1985) International Banking Survey, 16 March.

Eisenhardt, K M (1989) Agency Theory: An Assessment and Review. *Academy of Management Review*, 14, 57–74.

Elg, U (1998) The Role of Original Network Relations on the Extended Interorganizational Arena. *Fifth International Conference on Multi-Organisational Partnerships & Co-operative Strategy*. Conference paper, July. Balliol, Oxford.

Erden, D (1997) Stability and Satisfaction in Cooperative FDI: Partnerships in Turkey. In: *Cooperative Strategies: Asian Pacific Perspectives*, 158–83. Eds. Beamish, P W and Killing, J P. San Francisco: The New Lexington Press.

Faulkner, D (1995) *International Strategic Alliances: Co-operating to Compete.* London: McGraw-Hill.

Faulkner, D, Pitkethly, R and Child, J (1998) Change Processes in Multi-organisational Partnerships: Some National Comparisons. *Fifth International Conference on Multi-Organisational Partnerships & Co-operative Strategy.* Conference paper, July. Balliol, Oxford.

Florin, J M (1997) Organizing for Efficiency and Innovation: The Case of Nonequity Interfirm Cooperative Arrangements. In: *Cooperative Strategies: North American Perspectives*, 3–24. Eds. Beamish, P W and Killing, J P. San Francisco: The New Lexington Press.

Geringer, J M (1991) Strategic Determinants of Partner Selection Criteria in International Joint Ventures. *Journal of International Business Studies*, 22, 41–62.

Glaister, K W and Buckley, P J (1994) UK International Joint Ventures: An Analysis of Patterns of Activity and Distribution. *British Journal of Management*, 5(1), 33–51.

Glaister, K W and Buckley, P (1997) Task-related and Partner-related Selection Criteria in UK International Joint Ventures. *British Journal of Management*, 8, 199–222.

Glaister, K W, Husan, R and Buckley, P J (1998) UK International Joint Ventures with the Triad: Evidence for the 1990s. *British Journal of Management*, 9, 169–80.

Golden, B R (1997) Further Remarks on Retrospective Accounts in Organizational and Strategic Management Research. *The Academy of Management Journal*, 40(5), 1243–52.

Gomes-Casseres, B (1988) Joint Venture Cycles: The Evolution of Ownership Strategies of US MNEs, 1945–75. In: *Cooperative Strategies in International Business*, 111–28. Eds. Contractor, F J and Lorange, P. New York: Lexington Books.

Graham, J L (1988) Deference Given to the Buyer: Variations Across Twelve Cultures. In: *Cooperative Strategies in International Business*, 473–85. Eds. Contractor, F J and Lorange, P. New York: Lexington Books.

Gray, B and Yan, A (1997) Formation and Evolution of International Joint Ventures: Examples from US-Chinese Partnerships. In: *Cooperative Strategies: Asian Pacific Perspectives*, 57–88. Eds. Beamish, P W and Killing, J P. San Francisco: The New Lexington Press.

Green, R and Keogh, W (1998) Collaboration in the UK Upstream Oil and Gas Industry: Five Years On. *Fifth International Conference on Multi-Organisational Partnerships & Co-operative Strategy.* Conference paper, July. Balliol, Oxford.

Gulati, R (1998) Alliances and Networks. *Strategic Management Journal*, 19(4), 293–317.

Gulati, R (1999) Network Location and Learning: The Influence of Network Resources and Firm Capabilities on Alliance Formation. *Strategic Management Journal*, 20, 397–420.

Gulati, R, Noahria, N and Zaheer, A (2000a) Guest Editors' Introduction to the Special Issue: Strategic Networks. *Strategic Management Journal*, (Special Issue) 21(3), 199–201.

Gulati, R, Noahria, N and Zaheer, A (2000b) Strategic Networks. *Strategic Management Journal*, (Special Issue) 21(3), 203–15.

Ha[o]kansson, H and Johanson J (1988) Formal and Informal Cooperation Strategies in International Industrial Networks. In: *Cooperative Strategies in International Business*, 369–79. Eds. Contractor, F J and Lorange, P. New York: Lexington Books.

Hamel, G (1991) Competition for Competence and Inter-Partner Learning Within International Strategic Alliances. *Journal of International Business Studies*, **22**, 41–62.

Hamel, G and Prahalad, C-K (1994) *Competing for the Future*. Boston, Mass: Harvard Business School Press.

Harrigan, K R (1988a) Joint Ventures and Competitive Strategy. *Strategic Management Journal*, **9**, 141–58.

Harrigan, K R (1988b) Strategic Alliances and Partner Asymmetries. In: *Cooperative Strategies in International Business*, 205–26. Eds. Contractor, F J and Lorange, P. New York: Lexington Books.

Harzing, A-W (2002) *Journal Quality List*. Published on www.harzing.com

Hennart, J-F and Reddy, S (1997) The Choice Between Mergers/Acquisitions and Joint Ventures: The Case of Japanese Investors in the United States. *Strategic Management Journal*, **18**, 1–12.

Hennart, J-F and Reddy, S B (2000) Digestibility and Asymmetric Information in the Choice Between Acquisitions and Joint Ventures, Strategic Management Journal, **21** (2), 191–93.

Hennart, J-F, Kim, D-J and Zeng, M (1998) The Impact of Joint Venture Status on the Longevity of Japanese Stakes in US Manufacturing Affiliates. *Organization Science*, 9(3), 382–95.

Heracleous, L (1997) Strategic Thinking as Double-Loop Learning: Barrier and Facilitating Factors. *Faculty of Business Administration, National University of Singapore*, Research Paper Series: RPS #97–31.

Hærbert, L and Beamish, P (1997) Characteristics of Canada-Based International Joint Ventures. In: *Cooperative Strategies: North American Perspectives*, 403–27. Eds. Beamish, P W and Killing, J P. San Francisco: The New Lexington Press.

Hergert, M and Morris D (1988) Trends in International Collaborative Agreements. In: *Cooperative Strategies in International Business*, 99–109. Eds. Contractor, F J and Lorange, P. New York: Lexington Books.

Hitt, M A, Gimeno, J and Hoskisson, R E (1998) Current and Future Research Methods in Strategic Management. *Organisational Research Methods*, **1**(1), 6–44.

Hladik, K J (1988) R&D and International Joint Ventures. In: *Cooperative Strategies in International Business*, 187–203. Eds. Contractor, F J and Lorange, P. New York: Lexington Books.

Holm, D B, Eriksson, K and Johanson, J (1997) Business Networks and Cooperation in International Business Relationships. In: *Cooperative Strategies: Asian Pacific Perspectives*, 242–66. Eds. Beamish, P W and Killing, J P. San Francisco: The New Lexington Press.

Hopkins, W E and Hopkins, S A (1997) Strategic Planning – Financial Performance Relationships in Banks: A Causal Examination. *Strategic Management Journal*, **18**(8), 635–52.

Horton, V and Richey, B (1997) On Developing a Contingency Model of Technology Alliance Formation. In: *Cooperative Strategies: North American Perspectives*, 89–110. Eds. Beamish, P W and Killing, J P. San Francisco: The New Lexington Press.

Hoskins, C, McFadyen, S and Finn A (1997) A Comparison of the Motivation of Japanese and Canadian Participants in International Joint Ventures in Television and Film: The Role of Cultural Distance and Management Culture. In: *Cooperative Strategies: Asian Pacific Perspectives*, 157–77. Eds. Beamish, P W and Killing, J P. San Francisco: The New Lexington Press.

Hoskisson, R E, Hitt, M A, Wan, W P and Yin, D (1999) Theory and Research in Strategic Management: Swings of Pendulum. *Journal of Management*, **25**(3), 417–56.

Hull, F, Slowinski, G, Wharton, R and Azumi, K (1988) Strategic Partnerships Between Technological Entrepreneurs in the United States and Large Corporations in Japan and the United States. In: *Cooperative Strategies in International Business*, 445–56. Eds. Contractor, F J and Lorange, P. New York: Lexington Books.

Human, S E and Provan, K G (1997) An Emergent Theory of Structure and Outcomes in Small-Firm Strategic Manufacturing Networks. *The Academy of Management Journal*, **40**(2), 368–403.

Inkpen, A (1995) *The Management of International Joint Ventures: An Organizational Learning Perspective*. London: Routledge.

Inkpen, A C (1997) An Examination of Knowledge Management in International Joint Ventures. In: *Cooperative Strategies: North American Perspectives*, 337–69. Eds. Beamish, P W and Killing, J P. San Francisco: The New Lexington Press.

Inkpen, A C (1998) Learning and Knowledge Acquisition Through International Strategic Alliances. *The Academy of Management Executive*, **12**(4), 69–92.

Inkpen, A C (2000) A Note on the Dynamics of Learning Alliances: Competition, Cooperation, and Relative Scope. *Strategic Management Journal*, **21**(7), 775–79.

Inkpen, A C and Beamish, P W (1997) Knowledge, Bargaining Power, and the Instability of International Joint Ventures. *The Academy of Management Review*, **22**(1), 177–202.

Inkpen, A C and Currall, S C (1997) International Joint Venture Trust: An Empirical Examination. In: *Cooperative Strategies: North American Perspectives*, 308–34. Eds. Beamish, P W and Killing, J P. San Francisco: The New Lexington Press.

Inkpen, A C and Dinur, A (1998) Knowledge Management Processes and International Joint Ventures. *Organization Science*, **9**(4), 454–68.

Itschert, J and ul-Haq, R (2003) International Banking Strategic Alliances: Reflections on BNP/Dresdner. England and New York: Palgrave Macmillan.

Johanson, J and Matsson, L-G (1991) Interorganizational Relations in Industrial Systems: A Network Approach Compared with a Transaction-Cost Approach. In: *Markets, Hierarchies and Networks*, 256–64. Eds. Thompson, G, Frances, J, Levacic, R and Mitchell, J. London: Sage.

Johnson, G and Scholes, K (2002) *Exploring Corporate Strategy*. Pearson: England.

Johnson, J L, Cullen J B, Sakano, T and Takenouchi, H (1997) Setting the Stage for Trust and Strategic Integration in Japanese-US Cooperative Alliances. In: *Cooperative Strategies: North American Perspectives*, 227–54. Eds. Beamish, P W and Killing, J P. San Francisco: The New Lexington Press.

Johnson, J P (1997) Procedural Justice Perceptions Among International Joint Venture Managers: Their Impact on Organizational Commitment. In:

Cooperative Strategies: North American Perspectives, 197–226. Eds. Beamish, P W and Killing, J P. San Francisco: The New Lexington Press.

Jones, C, Hesterly, W S, Fladmoe-Lindquist, K and Borgatti, S P (1998) Professional Service Constellations: How Strategies and Capabilities Influence Collaborative Stability and Change. *Organization Science*, 9(3), 396–410.

Joshi, M P, Kashlak, R J and Sherman, H D (1998) How Alliances are Reshaping Telecommunications. *Long Range Planning*, 31(4), 542–48.

Kale, P, Singh, H and Perlmutter, H (2000) Learning and Protection of Proprietary Assets in Strategic Alliances: Building Relational Capital. *Strategic Management Journal*, (Special Issue) 21(3), 217–37.

Kalmbach Jr, C and Roussel, C (1999) Dispelling the Myths of Alliances. *Outlook Special Edition*, Andersen Consulting, October, 3–31.

Kaufman, A, Wood, C H and Theyle, G (2000) Collaboration and technology linkages: A strategic supplier typology. *Strategic Management Journal*, 21(6), 649–63.

Khanna, T (1998) The Scope of Alliances. *Organization Science*, 9(3), 340–55.

Khanna, T, Gulati, R and Nohria N (1998) The Dynamics of Learning Alliances: Competition, Cooperation, and Relative Scope. *Strategic Management Journal*, 19, 193–210.

Killing, J P (1988) Understanding Alliances: The Role of Task and Organizational Complexity. In: *Cooperative Strategies in International Business*, 55–67. Eds. Contractor, F J and Lorange, P. New York: Lexington Books.

Kogut, B (1988) A Study of the Life Cycle of Joint Ventures. In: *Cooperative Strategies in International Business*, 169–85. Eds. Contractor, F J and Lorange, P. New York: Lexington Books.

Kogut, B (2000) The Network as Knowledge: Generative Rules and the Emergence of Structure. *Strategic Management Journal*, (Special Issue) 21(3), 405–25.

Kogut, B, and Kulatilaka, N (2004) Real Options Pricing and Organisations: The Contingent Risks of Extended Theoretical Domains. *Academy of Management Review*, 29(1), 102–10.

Kogut, B and Singh H (1988) Entering the United States by Joint Venture: Competitive Rivalry and Industry Structure. In: *Cooperative Strategies in International Business*, 241–51. Eds. Contractor, F J and Lorange, P. New York: Lexington Books.

Koot, W T M (1988) Underlying Dilemmas in the Management of International Joint Ventures. In: *Cooperative Strategies in International Business*, 347–67. Eds. Contractor, F J and Lorange, P. New York: Lexington Books.

Korbin, S J (1988) Trends in Ownership of US Manufacturing Subsidiaries in Developing Countries: An Interindustry Analysis. In: *Cooperative Strategies in International Business*, 129–42. Eds. Contractor, F J and Lorange, P. New York: Lexington Books.

Koza, M P and Lewin, A Y (1998) The Co-evolution of Strategic Alliances. *Organization Science*, 9(3), 255–64.

Kumar, R and Nti, K O (1998) Differential Learning and Interaction in Alliance Dynamics: A Process and Outcome Discrepancy Model. *Organization Science*, 9(3), 356–67.

Kumar, S and Seth, A (1998) The Design of Coordination and Control Mechanisms for Managing Joint Venture-Parent Relationships. *Strategic Management Journal*, 19, 579–99.

Lane, F C (1985) Coins and Money of Account. Vol 1 of *Money and Banking in Medieval and Renaissance Venice*. Baltimore: London.

Lane, C (1998) Introduction. In: *Trust Within and Between Organizations*. Eds. Lane, C and Buckman, R. Oxford: Oxford University Press.

Larsson, R, Bengtsson, L, Henriksson, K and Sparks, J (1998) The Interorganizational Learning Dilemma: Collective Knowledge Development in Strategic Alliances. *Organization Science*, 9(3), 285–305.

Lawrence, P and ul-Haq, R (1997) Partner Selection Filters in Strategic Alliances in the European Banking Sector – Some Initial Observations. *Proceedings of the Seventh International Conference, Eastern Academy of Management International*, Conference Paper, June, Dublin.

Lawrence, P and ul-Haq, R (1998) Qualitative Research into Strategic Alliances. *Qualitative Market Research: An International Journal*, 1(1).

Lawson, T (1997) *Economics and Reality*. London: Routledge.

Lecraw, D J (1988) Countertrade: A Form of Cooperative International Business Arrangement. In: *Cooperative Strategies in International Business*, 425–42. Eds. Contractor, F J and Lorange, P. New York: Lexington Books.

Leung, K, Smith, P B, Wang, Z and Sun, H (1997) Job Satisfaction in Joint Venture Hotels in China: An Organizational Justice Analysis. In: *Cooperative Strategies: Asian Pacific Perspectives*, 226–44. Eds. Beamish, P W and Killing, J P. San Francisco: The New Lexington Press.

Leverick, F and Cooper, R (1998) Partnerships in the Motor Industry: Opportunities and Risks for Suppliers. *Long Range Planning*, 31(1), 72–81.

Lewicki, R J and Bunker, B B (1996) Developing and Maintaining Trust in Work Relationships. In: *Trust in Organisations: Frontiers of Theory and Research*, 114–39. Eds. Kramer, R M and Tyled, T R. Thousand Oaks, California: Sage.

Li, J and Shenkar, O (1997) The Perspectives of Local Partners: Strategic Objectives and Structure Preferences of International Cooperative Ventures in China. In: *Cooperative Strategies: Asian Pacific Perspectives*, 300–22. Eds. Beamish, P W and Killing, J P. San Francisco: The New Lexington Press.

Lin, J L, Yu, C-M and Seeto, D-H (1997) Motivations, Partners' Contributions, and Control of International Joint Ventures. In: *Cooperative Strategies: Asian Pacific Perspectives*, 115–34. Eds. Beamish, P W and Killing, J P. San Francisco: The New Lexington Press.

Lorange, P (1997) Black-Box Protection of Your Core Competencies in Strategic Alliances. In: *Cooperative Strategies: European Perspectives*, 59–73. Eds. Beamish, P W and Killing, J P. San Francisco: The New Lexington Press.

Lorange, P and Roos, J (1992) *Strategic Alliances: Formation, Implementation and Evolution*. Oxford: Blackwell.

Lu, Y and Björkman, I (1997) International Joint Venture Decision Making. In: *Cooperative Strategies: Asian Pacific Perspectives*, 3–21. Eds. Beamish, P W and Killing, J P. San Francisco: The New Lexington Press.

Lu, Y and Lake, D (1997) Managing International Joint Ventures: An Institutional Approach. In: *Cooperative Strategies: European Perspectives*, 74–99. Eds. Beamish, P W and Killing, J P. San Francisco: The New Lexington Press.

Luo, Y and Chen, M (1997) Business Strategy, Investment Strategy, and Performance of International Joint Ventures: The Case of China. In: *Cooperative Strategies: Asian Pacific Perspectives*, 341–74. Eds. Beamish, P W and Killing, J P. San Francisco: The New Lexington Press.

Lyles, M A (1988) Learning Among Joint Venture-Sophisticated Firms. In: *Cooperative Strategies in International Business*, 301–16. Eds. Contractor, F J and Lorange, P. New York: Lexington Books.

Lyles, M A and Salk, J E (1997) Knowledge Acquisition from Foreign Parents in International Joint Ventures: An Empirical Examination in the Hungarian Context. In: *Cooperative Strategies: Asian Pacific Perspectives*, 325–55. Eds. Beamish, P W and Killing, J P. San Francisco: The New Lexington Press.

Madhavan, R, Koka, B R and Prescott, J E (1998) Networks in Transition: How Industry Events (RE) Shape Interfirm Relationships. *Strategic Management Journal*, **19**, 439–59.

Madhok, A (1997) Economizing and Strategizing in Foreign Market Entry. In: *Cooperative Strategies: North American Perspectives*, 25–50. Eds. Beamish, P W and Killing, J P. San Francisco: The New Lexington Press.

Madhok, A and Tallman, S B (1998) Resources, Transactions and Rents: Managing Value Through Interfirm Collaborative Relationships. *Organization Science*, **9**(3), 326–39.

Makino, S and Beamish, P W (1999) Matching Strategy with the Choice of Ownership Structure: Japanese Joint Ventures in Asia. *The Academy of Management Executive*, **13**(4), 17–28.

Makino, S and Delios, A (1997) Local Knowledge Transfer and Performance: Implications for Alliance Formation in Asia. In: *Cooperative Strategies: Asian Pacific Perspectives*, 375–402. Eds. Beamish, P W and Killing, J P. San Francisco: The New Lexington Press.

Mason, J (1996) *Qualitative Researching*. London: Sage.

Mayrhofer, U (1997) Franco-British Strategic Alliances: A Contribution to the Study of Intra-European Partnerships. *The British Academy of Management, Annual Conference Paper*. September.

Medcof, J W (1997) Why Too Many Alliances End in Divorce. *Long Range Planning*, **30**(5), 718–32.

Merchant, H (1997) International Joint Venture Performance of Firms in the Nonmanufacturing Sector. In: *Cooperative Strategies: North American Perspectives*, 428–56. Eds. Beamish, P W and Killing, J P. San Francisco: The New Lexington Press.

Merchant, H and Schendal, D (2000) How Do International Joint Ventures Create Shareholder Value? *Strategic Management Journal*, **21**(7), 723–37.

Mintzberg, H, Raisinghand, D and Theoret, A (1976) The Structure of Unstructured Decision Processes. *Administrative Science Quarterly*, **21**, 246–75.

Mitchell, A (1998) Getting it Together – Strategic Alliances. *Marketing Business*, April, 18–23.

Mockler, R J (1997) Multinational Strategic Alliances: A Manager's Perspective. *Strategic Change*, **6**, 391–405.

Monge, P R, Fulk, J, Kalman, M E, Flanagin, A J, Parnassa, C and Rumsey, S (1998) Production of Collective Action in Alliance-Based Interorganizational Communication and Information Systems. *Organization Science*, **9**(3), 411–33.

Morison, I (1999) Changing Needs and Expectations. In: *Driving Strategic Change in Financial Services*, Ch 3. Eds: Taylor, B and Morison, I. Cambridge: Woodhead Publishing.

Moxon, R W, Roehl, T W and Truitt, J F (1988) International Cooperative Ventures in the Commercial Aircraft Industry: Gains, Sure, But What's My

Share? In: *Cooperative Strategies in International Business*, 255–77. Eds. Contractor, F J and Lorange, P. New York: Lexington Books.

Nair, A S and Stafford, E R (1998) Strategic Alliances in China: Negotiating the Barriers. *Long Range Planning*, 21(1), 139–46.

Naylor, J and Lewis, M (1997) Internal Alliances: Using Joint Ventures in a Diversified Company. *Long Range Planning*, 30(5), 678–88.

Nonaka, I and Takeuchi, H (1995) *The Knowledge Creating Company*, New York: Oxford University Press.

Nooteboom, B, Berger, H and Noorderhaven, N G (1997) Effects of Trust and Governance on Relational Risk. *The Academy of Management Journal*, 40(2), 308–38.

Nordberg, M, Campbell, A J and Verbeke, A (1997) Can Market-Based Contracts Substitute for Alliances in High-Technology Markets? In: *Cooperative Strategies: Asian Pacific Perspectives*, 356–75. Eds. Beamish, P W and Killing, J P. San Francisco: The New Lexington Press.

Nti, K O and Kumar, R (1998) Cost Reduction Learning and Competition in Strategic Alliances. *Fifth International Conference on Multi-Organisational Partnerships & Co-operative Strategy*. Conference paper, July. Balliol, Oxford.

Ocasio, W (1997) Towards an Attention-Based View of the Firm. *Strategic Management Journal*, 18, (Summer Special Issue), 187–206.

Olk, P (1997) The Effect of Partner Differences on the Performance of R&D Consortia. In: *Cooperative Strategies: North American Perspectives*, 133–59. Eds. Beamish, P W and Killing, J P. San Francisco: The New Lexington Press.

Olson, L B and Singsuwan, K (1997) The Effect of Partnership, Communication, and Conflict Resolution Behaviours on Performance Success of Strategic Alliances: American and Thai Perspectives. In: *Cooperative Strategies: Asian Pacific Perspectives*, 245–67. Eds. Beamish, P W and Killing, J P. San Francisco: The New Lexington Press.

Oman C P (1988) Cooperative Strategies in Developing Countries: The New forms of Investment. In: *Cooperative Strategies in International Business*, 383–402. Eds. Contractor, F J and Lorange, P. New York: Lexington Books.

Osborn, R N and Hagedoorn, J (1997) The Institutionalization and Evolutionary Dynamics of Interorganizational Alliances and Networks. *The Academy of Management Journal*, 40(2), 261–78.

Pan, Y (1997) The Formation of Japanese and US Equity Joint Ventures in China. *Strategic Management Journal*, 18(3), 247–54.

Pan, Y and Tse, D K (1997) Cooperative Strategies Between Foreign Firms in an Overseas Country. In: *Cooperative Strategies: Asian Pacific Perspectives*, 135–56. Eds. Beamish, P W and Killing, J P. San Francisco: The New Lexington Press.

Papanastassiou, M and Pearce, R (1997) Cooperative Approaches to Strategic Competitiveness Through MNE Subsidiaries: Insiders and Outsiders in the European Market. In: *Cooperative Strategies: Asian Pacific Perspectives*, 267–99. Eds. Beamish, P W and Killing, J P. San Francisco: The New Lexington Press.

Park, S H and Ungson, G R (1997) The Effect of National Culture, Organizational Complementarity, and Economic Motivation on Joint Venture Dissolution. *The Academy of Management Journal*, 40(2), 279–307.

Pearce, J L and Branyiczki, I (1997) Legitimacy: An Analysis of Three Hungarian-Western European Collaborations. In: *Cooperative Strategies: Asian Pacific*

Perspectives, 300–22. Eds. Beamish, P W and Killing, J P. San Francisco: The New Lexington Press.

Pearce, R J (1997) Towards Understanding Joint Venture Performance and Survival: A Bargaining and Influence Approach to Transaction Cost Theory. *The Academy of Management Review*, **22**(1), 203–25.

Perry, F E (1979) *A Dictionary of Banking*. Plymouth: Macdonald and Evans.

Perry, F E (1981) *The Elements of Banking*, 3rd ed. London: Methuen in association with the Institute of Bankers.

Pettigrew, A, Thomas, H and Whittington, R (2002) Strategic Management: The Strengths and Limitations of a Field. In: *Handbook of Strategy and Management*, 3–30. Eds. Pettigrew, A, Thomas, H and Whittington, R. London: Sage.

Pfeffer, J and Salanick, G R (1978) *The External Control of Organizations: A Resource Dependency Perspective*. New York: Harper and Row.

Phillips, M P, Pugh, D S (1994) *How To Get A PhD*. Buckingham: Open University Press.

Polanyi, K (1966) *The Tacit Dimension*. London: Routledge and Kegan Paul.

Porter, M E (1980) *Competitive Strategy*. New York: Free Press.

Porter, M E (1985) *Competitive Advantage: Creating and Sustaining Superior Performance*. New York: Free Press.

Porter, M E (1988) *Competitive Advantage of Nations*. New York: Free Press.

Pucik, V (1988) Strategic Alliances with the Japanese: Implications for Human Resource Management. In: *Cooperative Strategies in International Business*, 487–98. Eds. Contractor, F J and Lorange, P. New York: Lexington Books.

Pucik, V (1991) Technology Transfer in Strategic Alliances: Competition, Collaboration and Organizational Learning. In: *Technology Transfer in International Business*, 121–38. Eds. Agmon, T and von Glinow, M A. Oxford: Oxford University Press.

Punch, K (1998) *Introduction to Social Science Research: Quantitative and Qualitative Approaches*. London: Sage.

Ramanathan, K, Seth, A and Thomas, H (1997) Explaining Joint Ventures: Alternative Theoretical Perspectives. In: *Cooperative Strategies: North American Perspectives*, 51–85. Eds. Beamish, P W and Killing, J P. San Francisco: The New Lexington Press.

Rapaport, A (1961) *Fights, Games and Debates*. Ann Arbour Mich: University of Michigan Press.

Reuer, J J and Koza, M P (2000) Asymmetric Information and Joint Venture Performance: Theory and Evidence for Domestic and International Joint Ventures. *Strategic Management Journal*, **21**, 81–8.

Reuer, J J and Miller, K D (1997) Agency Costs and the Performance Implications of International Joint Venture Internalization. *Strategic Management Journal*, **18**(6), 425–38.

Ridley, M (1996) *The Origins of Virtue*. London: Viking.

Ring, P S (1997) Patterns of Process in Cooperative Interorganizational Relationships. In: *Cooperative Strategies: North American Perspectives*, 286–307. Eds. Beamish, P W and Killing, J P. San Francisco: The New Lexington Press.

Robins, J A, Tallman, S and Fladmoe-Lindquist, K (1998) Alliance Strategies for Emerging Economies: A Structural Approach to Autonomy and Dependence in US-Mexican Alliances. *Fifth International Conference on Multi-Organisational Partnerships & Co-operative Strategy*. Conference paper, July. Balliol, Oxford.

Root, F R (1988) Some Taxonomies of International Cooperative Arrangements. In: *Cooperative Strategies in International Business*, 69–80. Eds. Contractor, F J and Lorange, P. New York: Lexington Books.

Roussel, C J and Laird, R (1999) Minimalist or Invader: A Systematic View of Alliance Governance. *Outlook: Point of View*, No 99, Andersen Consulting.

Rowley, T, Behrens, D and Krackhardt, D (2000) Redundant Governance Structures: An Analysis of Structural and Relational Embeddedness in the Steel and Semiconductor Industries. *Strategic Management Journal*, (Special Issue) 21(3), 369–86.

Sainsburys Bank (2002) *Research Interview with D Bottom, Deputy CEO*. London.

Sarkar, M, Cavusgil, S T and Evirgen, C (1997) A Commitment-Trust Mediated Framework of International Collaborative Venture Performance. In: *Cooperative Strategies: North American Perspectives*, 255–85. Eds. Beamish, P W and Killing, J P. San Francisco: The New Lexington Press.

Saxton, T (1997) The Effects of Partner and Relationship Characteristics on Alliance Outcomes. *The Academy of Management Journal*, 40(2), 443–61.

Sayer, A (1992) *Method in Social Science: A Realist Approach*. London and New York: Routledge.

Schaan, J-L and Beamish, P W (1988) Joint Ventures General Managers in LDCs. In: *Cooperative Strategies in International Business*, 279–99. Eds. Contractor, F J and Lorange, P. New York: Lexington Books.

Schendal, D E and Hatten, K J (1972) Business Policy or Strategic Management: A Broader View for an Emerging Discipline. *Academy of Management Proceedings*, 99–102.

Sedaitis, J (1998) The Alliances of Spin-offs Versus Start-ups: Social Ties in the Genesis of Post-Soviet Alliances. *Organization Science*, 9(3), 368–81.

Si, S X and Bruton, G D (1999) Knowledge Transfer in International Joint Ventures in Transitional Economies: The China Experience. *The Academy of Management Executive*, 13(1), 83–90.

Simard, P (1996) *The Structuring of Cooperative Relationships*. First Year Report, Doctoral Studies. Judge Institute of Management Studies, University of Cambridge, June.

Simonin, B L (1997) The Importance of Collaborative Know-How: An Empirical Test of the Learning Organization. *The Academy of Management Journal*, 40(5), 1150–74.

Simonin, B L (1999) Ambiguity and the Process of Knowledge Transfer in Strategic Alliances. *Strategic Management Journal*, 20, 595–623.

Singh, K (1997) The Impact of Technological Complexity and Interfirm Cooperation on Business Survival. *The Academy of Management Journal*, 40(2), 339–67.

Singh, K and Mitchell, W (1996) Precarious Collaboration: Business Survival after Partners Shut Down or Form New Partnerships. *Strategic Management Journal*, 17, Special Issue, 99–115.

Sohn, J H D and Paik, Y (1997) Diversification as a Supplementary Means of Control in International Joint Ventures: The Case of Japanese MNCs in Korea. In: *Cooperative Strategies: Asian Pacific Perspectives*, 268–99. Eds. Beamish, P W and Killing, J P. San Francisco: The New Lexington Press.

Stabell, C B and Fjeldstad Ø D (1998) Configuring Value for Competitive Advantage: On Chains, Shops, and Networks. *Strategic Management Journal*, 19, 413–37.

Stiles, J (1997) Managing Strategic Alliance Success: Determining the Influencing Factors of Intent Within the Partnership. *Henley Management College,* Working Paper Series: HWP 9721.

Stiles, J (1999) Co-operative/Competitive Influences on Network Partnerships in the Airline Industry. *International Forum on Strategic Management,* Newsletter, No 17, August, 9–15. Henley Management College.

Stuart, T E (2000) Interorganizational Alliances and the Performance of Firms: A Study of Growth and Innovation Rates in a High-Technology Industry. *Strategic Management Journal,* 21(8), 791–811.

Sulej, J C (1998) Strategic Structure and Orientation in UK/International Equity Joint Ventures. *Fifth International Conference on Multi-Organisational Partnerships & Co-operative Strategy.* Conference paper, July. Balliol, Oxford.

Swan, P F and Ettlie, J E (1997) US-Japanese Manufacturing Equity Relationships. *The Academy of Management Journal,* 40(2), 462–79.

Sydow, J and Windeler, A (1998) Organizing and Evaluating Interfirm Networks: A Structurationist Perspective on Network Processes and Effectiveness. *Organization Science,* 9(3), 265–84.

Tallman, S, Sutcliffe, A G and Antonian, B A (1997) Strategic and Organizational Issues in International Joint Ventures in Moscow. In: *Cooperative Strategies: Asian Pacific Perspectives,* 184–211. Eds. Beamish, P W and Killing, J P. San Francisco: The New Lexington Press.

Taylor, B (1999) The Darwinian Shakeout in Financial Services. *International Forum on Strategic Management,* Newsletter, No 16, April, 4–8. Henley Management College.

Tiemessen, I, Lane, H W, Crossan, M M and Inkpen A C (1997) Knowledge Management in International Joint Ventures. In: *Cooperative Strategies: North American Perspectives,* 370–99. Eds. Beamish, P W and Killing, J P. San Francisco: The New Lexington Press.

Toral, L (2000) *International Joint Ventures: Managerial Lessons to Draw from European-Argentine Partnerships.* Unpublished doctoral thesis, Université de Neuchâtel.

Tyebjee T T (1988) Japan's Joint Ventures in the United States. In: *Cooperative Strategies in International Business,* 457–72. Eds. Contractor, F J and Lorange, P. New York: Lexington Books.

Tyler, B B and Steensma, H K (1998) The Effects of Executives' Experiences and Perceptions in Their Assessment of Potential Technological Alliances. *Strategic Management Journal,* 19(7), 939–65.

ul-Haq, R, Hamilton R and Morison I (1996) Strategic Alliances – An Alternative Schema. *Journal of Financial Abstracts: Series A, Corporate Finance and Organisations.* Working Paper Series, 2(26a) (Electronic Journal), 1–2, 5–6.

Villinger, R (1996) Post-Acquisition Managerial Learning in Central East Europe. *Organization Studies,* 17, 181–206.

Walker, G (1988) Network Analysis for Cooperative Interfirm Relationships. In: *Cooperative Strategies in International Business,* 227–40. Eds. Contractor, F J and Lorange, P. New York: Lexington Books.

Wernerfelt, B (1984) A Resource Based Theory of the Firm. *Strategic Management Journal,* 5, 171–80.

Westney, D E (1988) Domestic and Foreign Learning Curves in Managing International Cooperative Strategies. In: *Cooperative Strategies in International*

Business, 339–46. Eds. Contractor, F J and Lorange, P. New York: Lexington Books.

Whipp, R (1996) Creative Deconstruction: Strategy and Organisation. In *Handbook of Organization Studies*, 261–75. Eds. Clegg, S R, Hardy, G and Nord, W R. London: Sage.

Williamson, O E (1982) *Markets and Hierarchies: Analysis and Antitrust Implications: A study in the Economics of Internal Organisation.* USA: Macmillan.

Williamson, O E (1985) *The Economic Institutions of Capitalism.* New York: Free Press.

Williamson, O E (1986) *Economic Organisations: Firms, Markets, and Policy Control.* New York: Free Press.

Williamson, O E (1970) *Corporate Control and Business Behaviour.* USA: Prentice Hall.

Yeung, H W (1997) Cooperative strategies and Chinese Business Networks: A Study of Hong Kong Transnational Corporations in the ASEAN Region. In: *Cooperative Strategies: Asian Pacific Perspectives*, 22–56. Eds. Beamish, P W and Killing, J P. San Francisco: The New Lexington Press.

Zajac, E J (1998) Commentary on 'Alliances and Networks' by R Gulati. *Strategic Management Journal*, **19**, 319–21.

Zucker, L G (1986) Production of Trust: Institutional Sources of Economic Structure, 1840–1920. *Research in Organization Behaviour*, **8**, 53–111.

Index

Note: Page numbers in italics refer to tables, figures